SURVIVING ZOMBIE WARFARE

CUSTOMIZE YOUR RIDE FOR A
ZOMBIE WAR ZONE

SEAN T. PAGE

This edition published in 2019 by:

The Rosen Publishing Group, Inc.
29 East 21st Street
New York, NY 10010

Cataloging-in-Publication Data

Names: Page, Sean T.
Title: Customize your ride for a zombie warzone / Sean T. Page.
Description: New York : Rosen YA, 2019. | Series: Surviving zombie warfare
| Includes glossary and index.
Identifiers: ISBN 9781508186441 (pbk.) | ISBN 9781508186465 (library bound)
Subjects: LCSH: Zombies—Juvenile literature. | Survival—Juvenile literature.
| Emergency management—Juvenile literature.
| Automobiles—Customizing—Juvenile literature.
Classification: LCC PN6231.Z65 P345 2019 | DDC 818'.602—dc23
Manufactured in the United States of America

Originally published in English by Haynes Publishing under the title:
Zombie Survival Transport Manual © Sean T. Page 2017.

MINISTRY OF ZOMBIES

CONTENTS

MOTORIZED TRANSPORT — 6

CONVERTING YOUR CAR — 8
VEHICLE INTERIOR — 10
ENGINE AND MECHANICS — 12
FITTED WEAPONS — 14
ON-BOARD WEAPONS — 16
THE PERFECT ZOMBIE APOCALYPSE VEHICLE — 18
FUEL FOR SURVIVORS — 20
THE POST-APOCALYPTIC GARAGE — 22
ZOMBIE APOCALYPSE RV — 24
ZOMBIE BATTLE BUS — 26

MOTORCYCLE OPTIONS — 28

ZOMBIES AND MOTORCYCLES — 30

POST-APOCALYPTIC DRIVING — 32

CONTEXT AND ENVIRONMENT — 34
ZOMBIE AWARENESS — 36
HIDDEN DANGERS — 38
HOSTILE HUMANS — 40
SURVIVOR GROUPS — 42

GLOSSARY — 44
FOR FURTHER READING — 45
FOR MORE INFORMATION — 45
INDEX — 47

AUTHOR'S ACKNOWLEDGEMENTS

There were many experts involved in this book and I would like to particularly thank Steve "Rusty" Langdon for answering endless questions about his wasteland scooter and his war stories. To Mrs Eileen Cassidy, for travelling to London on several occasions and for allowing us to print plans to her apocalypse shopping cart. To Toyota, Honda, Hyundai, and the RAC, who provided some of the motoring inspiration for this volume. To all the survivors who kindly contributed their vehicle plans and case studies for inclusion – we couldn't fit them all in but they all proved to be invaluable to our research. Finally, to my partners in crime – Ian, Louise, and Richard – for their belief that such a book is essential to help protect the country and for settling the regrettable incident with the flame thrower out of court. Above all, to my wife Constance and daughter Nikita, who is currently converting her trike into a devastating wasteland cruiser.

POST-APOCALYPTIC SOUNDTRACK

Music is going to be even more important after the zombie apocalypse. With radio and TV stations off the air, you'll be depending on your in-vehicle entertainment to keep you occupied so don't get left with a Genesis mixtape someone made in 1989.

On the subject of formats, some may snigger at the idea of audio tapes but survival experts do not generally rate the survival chances of many digital forms of music. It's possible that your illegally downloaded MP3 collection could survive if you have the right technical set up but most advise audio tapes as your base storage unit.

Music choice will be as diverse as vehicle type in the wasteland but it is important, as the music you play sets the scene for your post-apocalyptic persona. For example, if you wish to transform from an under-paid office drone into a chopper riding, poncho-wearing survivor of the apocalypse, you need to ensure that you have the right sounds to back you up. As we couldn't be bothered to dig out every 'hard man' track for you (well, you have to do something), we've included the perfect post-apocalyptic mixtape track list to help get you started.

Beware that the playing of any loud music will attract zombies – that is apart from the Bucks Fizz track – for some reason, the dead find this particular track repellent for reasons unknown to current science.

A End of the World Mix

90

TAPE 1 NORMAL POSITION   NORMAL BIAS 120 µs EQ

Track list

The End of the World
Skeeter Davis (1962)

Highway to Hell
AC/DC (1979)

Armageddon It
Def Leppard (1987)

Waiting for the End of the World
Elvis Costello (1977)

The Beginning of the End
Rob Zombie (1998)

Making Your Mind Up
Bucks Fizz (1981)

(Don't Fear) The Reaper
Blue Oyster Cult (1976)

It's the End of the World
as we Know It (And I feel Fine)
R.E.M (1987)

The Last Night on Earth
Green Day (2009)

Bermuda Triangle
Barry Manilow (1981)

A Visit to a Sad Planet
Leonard Nimoy (1967)

Bad Moon Rising
Creedance Clearwater Revival (1969)

MOTORIZED TRANSPORT

While there are plenty of non-motorized transport options available, let's face it – who really wants to face the end of the world on a pair of roller skates or a scooter? The real action in the wasteland will be motorized.

Keeping and maintaining a car or other motorized vehicle could give you a real edge in the chaos – hopefully, your survival studies so far have demonstrated that. You'll be able to escape the city, forage further, and outrun other hopeless and desperate survivors. This section looks at motorized prepping with particular reference to creating a safe location for your vehicle and includes detailed plans on converting the 'average family car' into a post-apocalyptic road warrior machine. Many of the guidelines are equally applicable to other vehicle types so feel free to adapt and develop your own ideas as far as your budget and skills will allow. Technology is consumer demand driven so we now regularly see innovative cross-overs in the marketplace such as

expensive branded luxury cars that have impressive off-road credentials, including full 4 wheel drive, despite never leaving the city.

In reality, it would be impossible to include every possible configuration of motorized transport in this manual so we will start with a broad survey of car-type vehicles before looking at larger vehicles such as vans and buses later in the volume. For now, let's review the most common types of vehicles found on our roads such as sports, passenger, classic, and the growing category of sports utility vehicles, as well as hardy pickup trucks and flexible people carriers.

OPTION 1
SPORTS CARS

High performance sports and soft top 2 seaters won't survive long in the wastelands. They may look the business and, for sure, the end of the world is the time to snag a test drive from that deserted supercar showroom in Mayfair, but that's all it will be – a short test drive. Delicate, highly tuned engines, extremely low ground-clearance and poor storage – there's not much for a serious zombie prepper to love here. Blocked and uneven roads will negate the only advantage they do offer – their exceptional acceleration and speed.

 You may occasionally see them driven by warlords as trophies and demonstrations of power but apart from that, they'll disappear pretty quickly. Plus, driving an open top car during a zombie outbreak is like sticking a sign on your head saying 'please eat me'.

OPTION 2
FAMILY HATCHBACKS

Lists like this can sometimes seem like a catalogue selection from which you select the right option for you and to some extent this is the case. But, for many, the humble family car will be their vehicle of choice for obvious reasons. One of these is that it's one of the most common car types on the road and this means most survivors will be familiar with the layout and operation. They're also a good balance of storage, passenger space and power. However, modern family cars are designed for tarmac roads and often perform badly off-road or in poor road conditions.

 This broad group of vehicles will be the choice of thousands of survivors but it's important to look at some of the adaptations reviewed in this book to turn a reasonable zombie survival car into a hardened zombie-proof Bug-Out Vehicle.

OPTION 3
EMERGENCY VEHICLES

A wide range of options, some with the mouth-watering prospect of firearms and other specialist equipment you can turn on the walking dead. At the end of the world, who would pass up the opportunity to grab an emergency vehicle and 'blue light' it through the wasteland? There are some serious choices here in terms of ambulances, police cars and even SWAT team vehicles. Many models are adapted for emergency conditions and don't overlook the well-equipped command and control vehicles.

 First things first – if an emergency vehicle is still in use you must leave it. Many first-responders will be desperately battling to save humanity; the last thing they want is their vehicle getting stolen or looted. Wait to find an abandoned model.

MOTORIZED TRANSPORT
THE ROAD, LAW AND ZOMBIES

Much of the advice in this manual focuses on vehicle choice and careful preparation – but what if you find yourself without transport during a zombie outbreak? The Ministry of Zombies asked a prominent expert about the legalities of procuring transport during a crisis.

▶ The first consideration must be whether the governing authority has declared an official state of emergency. If this has been done, then the standard UN rules around the legality of foraging apply.

▶ Secondly, is whether procuring a vehicle from a zombie constitutes legal theft – in many legal codes around the world a human turned into a zombie is still, at least legally, considered to be alive. If you find the perfect vehicle with a zombie inside, then you deal with the zombie and make off with the said vehicle, you could be guilty of theft.

All clear? In reality, the legal guidelines around a major zombie outbreak are complex and unclear. Far better to be prepared but if you do find yourself in dire straits remember to forage only what you need to get back to your home base, do no harm to your fellow survivors and be wary of rogues or bandits posing as police or other authorities.

OPTION 4
SUVs

Sports Utility Vehicles (SUVs) now dominate our roads, with some models offering car-like levels of comfort with real off-road capability. A solid 4WD version from a good manufacturer is a superb base for your zombie survival planning. SUVs are hard wearing, have good storage, and a high driving position – all good assets for apocalyptic driving. Not the best fuel economy – some models are prone to tipping over – and be cautious of models which are designed to have the 'look' of an SUV but come with no off-road capability.

 An SUV or Jeep is a very practical choice but be wary as not all SUV's are the same. Many preppers favor slightly older models, which deliver a rougher ride but have less of the on-board technology disliked by serious survivalists.

OPTION 5
PICKUP TRUCKS

Hardy workhorses, designed for tough conditions – what's not to love? Superb build quality, decent off-road capability, and ample storage. Basic models are tough enough, although many lack the comforts of a car, but top-level models are possibly the best production model vehicles for the end of the world. The Toyota Hilux Invincible rules the pickup world. There is little this vehicle cannot do. Technology levels are creeping up on these vehicles so older models may be easy to maintain. Source an older model in good condition if you can.

 Later in this volume, we'll take a look at commercial vehicles as potential Bug- Out options. Many light commercial vehicles share the same features as pickup trucks but for many reasons, pickups seem to be the vehicle of choice for hardcore preppers.

OPTION 6
PEOPLE CARRIERS

Most frequently seen on the school run, these vehicles are often referred to by preppers as Road Utility Vehicles or RUVs. There are countless variations and makes, from smaller 6-seaters all the way up to converted commercial vehicle minibuses. Their obvious strength is storage space and the capacity to transport a group in one. Add to this that many models offer good performance and fuel economy. The downside is off-road performance with most production models managing very poorly on anything other than smooth tarmac roads.

 Standard models offer excellent storage capacity and should be considered if you plan to make your daily use car into your Bug-Out Vehicle. Shares many of the limitations of a family car in terms of going off-road.

MOTORIZED TRANSPORT

CONVERTING YOUR CAR

One of the more frequent questions asked on zombie prepper forums is "How can I prepare my car for the zombie apocalypse?" The query is often followed up with the information that many people only have one car and that it's used for the daily school run. So, how can you practically prepare your vehicle?

1 TIME AND RESOURCES

From that first moment when you wake up to find slobbering zombies at your window to when you're a fully prepared zombie prepper, time and resources are a key consideration. How serious are you about zombie prepping? What kind of money and time are you prepared to put into staying safe?

2 VEHICLE SELECTION

You may own a battle-equipped Humvee or a 2001 Rover which is forever breaking down – you need to get the core right if you are going to invest in your vehicle. How robust is your current vehicle? Is it suitable as a framework for your anti-zombie preparation plans?

3 DEFENSIVE ARMOR

Selecting the right armor to defend your vehicle is vital – fit a fully high-tech armor plate to resist any raiders or use chicken wire across the windows. Are you prepared to be known as the village nutcase if you fit a steel grill across your windscreen? Heavy armor can also impact on fuel efficiency – have you budgeted for this?

4 WEAPONS AND ARMAMENT

Known as "tooling up" in the prepper community, it could be using anything from a spare M60 you had lying around the garage to a box of plastic forks that were left over after Grandad's 70th. Do you understand what you can legally do in terms of adding weapons to your vehicle? Are you confident you can handle any new firepower that you fit?

This schematic overviews the key anti-zombie and apocalypse features which can be fitted to a standard family car. It outlines the main zones of operation when it comes to fixtures and fittings which will help you stay alive in the wasteland.

FENDERS, HOOD

There are many options to strengthen your front corners, particularly if you plan to hit a lot of zombies – consider wrapping with bull bars and additional soldered plates. The hood can be used as a weapons platform but fitting is considerably more complicated than roof versions. Some preppers simply cover their hood with small sandbags to protect the engine area.

DOORS

Modern car doors are sufficient to keep out the walking dead but you may want to strengthen in case of any road war damage – consider collision shields, welded plates, or spikes. It is important that your vehicle has an alternative escape route other than the 2–4 main doors, perhaps through the trunk or out of the top.

ROOF

Often referred to as "the deck" in zombie vehicle prepping circles – ensure that you have a properly constructed hatch whether you plan to use it for observation, escape or as a weapons platform – consider adding mounted weapons, directional lights, and zombie-whistles. Also a useful location for storage.

WHEELS AND ARCHES

A protective skirt around your wheel arches is a good investment and can be relatively easy to fit. In some cases, these can be fitted to almost cover the wheel. In terms of tires, consider an apocalypse-grade tire. Opinion is divided on the subject of wheel blades – with many survivors saying that they are more dangerous to your own party than the walking dead. Still, it would look cool to have great foot-long blades spinning from the wheels.

COLOR

Are zombies color sensitive? The medical evidence is inconclusive but what evidence we do have suggests they are drawn to brighter colors. Also, think hiding in an urban landscape, not sticking out. Look at dark colors, greys, mottled and dirty, painted on rust – urban camouflage means you won't be an obvious target.

FRONT GRILL

Many SUVs already have them but your front bumper needs to be replaced by a full-range bull bar system. Look out for a modern polyethylene one which is still hardy enough for zombie bashing but will offer some spring and deflect defence in the event of a collision. The front of your vehicle will certainly require protection in this area. It is not unheard of for a particularly sharp fragment of zombie bone to pierce the grill of a regular car and do some serious damage, so defend your front.

WINDSHIELD

Modern windscreens are strong but this area should still be protected by some form of cage. Ensure that it doesn't block your wipers and consider fitting improved blades to help you clear the excessive zombie matter from the screen. Halfords will be selling a "zombie-cleaning" screen wash from 2020 onwards but you'll need to order specialist screen wash online until then – choose the purple-colored ZombAway screen wash.

OTHER WINDOWS

Modern vehicle glass is strong enough to resist zombies but you may still want to supplement it with steel mesh. If you are going for full armor then consider bulletproof glass or steel shutters. Darkened glass can help avoid any unwanted zombie attention plus gives you that 'street gangsta' look.

GENERAL ARMOR

There are various levels of car armor so get some specialist advice. B4 or B6 ballistic protection levels will be sufficient for most hostile wasteland encounters. Many preppers defend key areas so as not to overload the vehicle. It's not cheap to armor up a car.

VEHICLE INTERIOR

Maintaining your vehicle's interior systems, such as your on-board Bug-Out Supply, which will help keep you mobile and alive in the wasteland, is a core requirement – never overlook it! Think of the interior of your vehicle as your mobile survival space. It's the location you will come to rely on for keeping the supplies and weapons that will keep you alive. In truth, you could fill a whole volume on both topics but in this section, we'll just do a quick survey of the key issues and challenges.

There are various techniques for creating additional space in an average car, the most obvious being to remove any unnecessary seating, particularly at the rear. With new models, vehicle designers go to great lengths to create unique vehicle interiors and most lack configurable options – for example, central consoles can rarely be moved as they conceal crucial electrical or mechanical components vital to the car's functioning. Realistically, any work beyond seat removal or creating interior access to the trunk could end up more costly than just buying a more suitable Bug-Out Vehicle.

▶ BUG-OUT VEHICLE TRUNK

The list included here is very much an idealised Bug-Out Trunk example. Does your on-board Bug-Out Kit need to be in the trunk? No. We have already looked at the option of using a trailer but, for most people, the trunk is a logical location. Remember, Bug-Out supplies are a personal choice but should contain everything you need to stay on the road and survive. You will most likely need to re-work the following suggestions based on factors such as the size of your vehicle and group, your budget, and any legal requirements.

> ⚠ **IMPORTANT**
>
> **ALWAYS ADHERE TO THE CURRENT LAWS AND REGULATIONS AROUND ROAD VEHICLE WORTHINESS, INSURANCE AND THE CARRYING OF WEAPONS. IT'S POINTLESS CREATING YOUR DREAM ZOMBIE APOCALYPSE VEHICLE FROM GRANDMA'S OLD COROLLA ONLY TO HAVE IT SEIZED BY THE FEDS BEFORE THE DEAD RISE. BE DISCREET. GET YOURSELF EDUCATED AND STAY LEGAL.**

1 FULL-SIZED SPARE TIRE

Forget space-saving alternatives, a full-sized spare tire with the appropriate floor jack is an essential component in any on-board Bug-Out Supplies. A flat or punctured tire is possibly the top reason for vehicle breakdown so be prepared with the parts, tools, and the skills to complete a change. You should be able to change your vehicle's tire in less than 10 minutes.

2 DRINKING WATER/PURIFICATION KIT

Again, a vital part of any kit. Experts suggest at least a gallon a day per survivor of drinking water, supported by purification kits and tablets. Commercially bottled mineral water will last about 3 years but most hardcore survivalists prefer to bottle their own in bulk containers adding a preservative such as tiny quantities of household bleach. You should only use this technique once you are confident in your own survival skills.

3 FUEL SUPPLIES

It is a golden rule to always keep your vehicle fuel tank full. You should also keep on-board supplies in purpose-built cans. Consider the use of preservatives such as fuel stabilizers to increase the longevity of your fuel and keep your stocks in rotation. Writing dates clearly on cans will help with this.

4 EMERGENCY BUG-OUT BAG

If you have less than a minute to abandon your vehicle or if it breaks down and you have to get out in a hurry, this is the backpack you grab. 72 hours of essential supplies in a light-weight back pack. Grab it, grab your weapon and get your skates on. Remember that you may be able to return to your vehicle once it's safe to do so to forage more supplies.

5 WEAPONS CACHE

Every survivor on-board will be carrying weapons so this is your extra cache of weapons and ammunition. Our illustration shows an adapted AK-47z assault rifle plus side arms. Where firearms are restricted for legal reasons, consider pepper spray, baseball bats, police-style batons. Weapons mix is a personal choice so consider those in your party and your defence requirements.

6 ALTERNATIVE TRANSPORT

In our example, there's an inflatable boat as an alternative Bug-Out Vehicle. This is a practical choice as it doesn't take up much room and is particularly useful where the collapse of civilization has led to wide scale flooding. Other interior solutions could include folding bicycles or small handcarts, the latter being used to ferry supplies away from an abandoned vehicle.

MOTORIZED TRANSPORT
INTERIOR CABIN

Everything inside your vehicle must justify its space so strip back on any unnecessary gadgets and electrics. You need as much space as possible for armed crew, weapons, and any supplies. If you don't need all the seats, consider removing them. Many preppers have their vehicle strengthened with internal support bars, to create a strong crash-proof cage inside. Don't forget some secret compartments for essentials.

Most survivalists create a system with their full Bug-Out supplies in the boot and with further smaller bags or kits inside the cabin. This decision depends on many factors including the vehicle and your plans once the walking dead arrive. There are any number of accessories you can spend your survival budget on to enhance your vehicle such as military grade navigation systems with pre-downloaded maps, encrypted two-way radios but don't overlook a good library of national maps and a compass. Check any decent survival forum for hundreds of posts on the various bits of post-apocalyptic technology now out there on the market.

7 SLEEPING BAG AND TEMPORARY SHELTER

This set of items should be scaled according to the size of your party. For sure, a 5-seasons sleeping bag with a good-sized green plastic sheet is the minimum. If you have the space, add in more plastic sheets with rope.

8 CONCEALED STORAGE SPACE

Some vehicles have useful under-trunk storage areas. It's worth sourcing a Bug-Out Vehicle with this feature as it can be used to store anything you want to be over-looked by a quick and opportunistic thief. Some preppers install booby traps inside these areas.

9 SEALED CONTAINERS

Tough plastic containers are excellent locations in which to store emergency rations as well any other emergency kit such as fire lighting equipment and cooking utensils. There is vast wealth of information out there about Bug-Out food selections but obviously long-duration is a key factor. There is also a debate on the use of ready-to-eat emergency rations, which are widely used in the military and take up minimal space.

10 MEDICAL KIT

Again, plenty of discussion on the content of an Emergency Bug-Out Kit but remember to get the training to support anything you include. A basic kit should have basic medical supplies but also personal hygiene products such as antibacterial wet wipes, which can help reduce the chances of infection, and any prescription medicines you need. An emergency dental kit is also worth investigating.

11 SPARES AND PARTS

Tires and jacks have already been mentioned but the list of what to include is still endless – consider spare batteries, jump cables, basic tools, fuses, fan belts, and fluids. It's also worth including emergency lighting and the relevant Haynes car manual, along with any other survival material you can't live without.

MOTORIZED TRANSPORT

ENGINE AND MECHANICS

Experts often refer to keeping your vehicle in good working order and, in this sense, preparing your vehicle for the zombie apocalypse is no exception – every vehicle be it a car, SUV, or motorcycle requires regular maintenance, particularly to core drive areas, such as the engine. Running out of fuel, an over-heated engine or even a flat battery are no longer minor inconveniences in the wasteland – these kind of vehicle issues could get you eaten. Whilst it may be tempting to start steel meshing windows and fitting killer zombie bull bars to the front of your car, never overlook the maintenance of these parts of your vehicle.

In terms of car performance, preparing a Bug-Out Vehicle is less about delicate fine-tuning to improve acceleration or top speed and more about ensuring you get the best fuel economy possible, that your engine continues to function and there is less wear on components such as tires. One important factor to consider, and which runs counter to some of the survival features reviewed in this book, is assessing your vehicle's ideal weight – strip out any unnecessary clutter and weight to maximize your MPG. It's remarkable how often vehicles fitted with the latest anti-zombie weapons breakdown at survival training events for reasons linked to a simple lack of maintenance. Keep your car healthy with the best oil, quality air filters, regularly changed spark plugs, and the best tires you can afford.

MOTORIZED TRANSPORT
VEHICLE CHECKS

Remember the basics from your zombie survival training – keep the fluids and fuel full; keep the engine and mechanics well-maintained; regularly check for any blockages, particularly as zombie gunk tends to bung up filters. Maintaining your vehicle can be summarized using the acronym FITBOW – these go beyond just considering the engine so it's best to think of FITBOW as a complete check of the automotive survival system rather than just a basic engine check.

FLUIDS
Fuel, windscreen washer (zombie variant if possible), and coolant. Basic stuff but the cause of many breakdowns if not regularly checked, particularly if you've been under fire.

INTERIOR
Basic check on Bug-Out Supplies – is everything full and in date? Are your weapons clean and maintained? Is your interior clean, tidy, and secure?

ALWAYS KEEP YOUR VEHICLE WELL-MAINTAINED, SERVICED, AND FULLY FUELED. NO ONE WANTS A VEHICLE BREAK DOWN JUST AS THE HORDE IS DESCENDING.

TIRES
Check pressure and your spare. Look out for

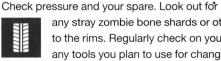

any stray zombie bone shards or other damage to the rims. Regularly check on your jack and any tools you plan to use for changing a wheel.

BASHERS
Bashers is a term mainly used in the US to refer

to any fixed or on-board weapons. If you've fitted a frontal grill, is it fixed and firmly held in place? Check any anti-zombie weapons such as decomposition filters etc.

OIL

Oil should get a special mention. In reality, survivors are good at checking fuel levels but they forget to check their oil. Easy to check and easy to top up but let it run down or get a leak and miss it and you can do irreparable damage to your vehicle.

WINDOWS

Check for cracks and that any steel mesh is firmly in place. Keep your windows clear and clean. Zombie gunk from creatures you run down will smother your windscreen, blocking your view and leaving masses of infected material on the vehicle. Clean it down with watered-down bleach before using any window cleaning products.

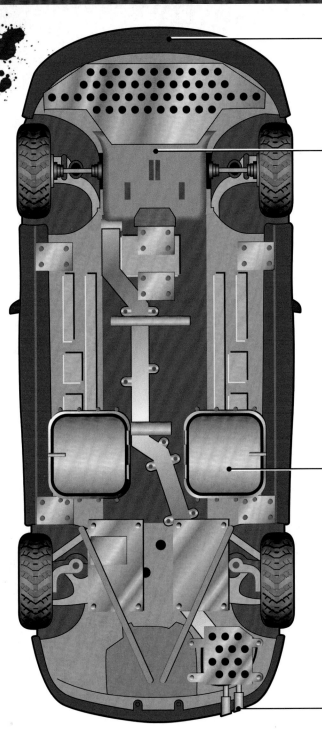

GROUND CLEARANCE

You need good ground clearance for any off-road driving and many preppers opt to support this by insisting that their Bug-Out Vehicle is a robust 4WD model.

SHIELDING

It is possible to shield the underside of your vehicle and therefore reduce both the number of grab points for zombies and off-road damage by fitting steel skid plates. Not all experts agree on the need for under-body armor.

ESCAPE HATCH

Fitting a vehicle floor exit hatch is a major adjustment but can be worth it on a larger vehicle. On smaller vehicles, survivors tend to look at the cheaper option of escaping through the back seat and the trunk. Also, as any automotive engineer will tell you, unless professionally done, any structural alterations to your vehicle will affect the strength of the car-frame – most of which are now in a unibody construction format. Basically, you don't want to make any changes that could weaken your vehicle in the event of a roll-over or if you are planning to add body armor or weapons.

"END OF THE WORLD" EXHAUST

Your exhaust system needs some special attention for two reasons. Firstly, from a defensive perspective, it will need reinforcing or a combination of grabbing zombies and off-road driving will take its toll. Secondly, going on the offensive, it is worth fitting a decomposition kit weapon system to your vehicle. Both adjustments will cost money but are very worthwhile investments. Beyond this, a regular maintenance routine should be in place to monitor the system and check on noise levels. Most serious zombie preppers keep a complete spare exhaust system in their fortified garage. It's a relatively inexpensive insurance policy against any major issues.

REMEMBER
Excessive noise from a poorly maintained vehicle or a noisy diesel engine will attract the dead from every street corner. All engines make noise but in zombie survival terms – the quieter the better.

"ADDING ANY PLATE ARMOR UNDERNEATH YOUR VEHICLE WILL ADD WEIGHT AND ISN'T ALWAYS EFFECTIVE. THE REAL ANSWER TO BETTER OFF-ROAD PERFORMANCE IS GETTING GOOD GROUND CLEARANCE, YOUR APPROACH AND DEPARTURE ANGLES RIGHT, PLENTY OF LOW END TORQUE, AND THE RIGHT TIRES."
TONY "WINKLE" HODGETTS, FORMER RAC PATROLMAN AND ZOMBIE SURVIVALIST

13

FITTED WEAPONS

It's incorrect to define "fitted weapons" as permanent on-board fixtures to your vehicle as in practice many can be removed if need be. For example, if you are forced to abandon your perfect zombie Bug-Out Vehicle, you can still detach the specially configured M60z you mounted on the roof, providing that you can carry it. However, there is permanence around many fitted weapons, particularly the offensive capability items, such as fixed front guns and rear-flame tail guns. There are also important legal regulations to consider. Under current law, you cannot equip your vehicle with any of the weapons mentioned in this manual – bar having a bag of baseball bats in the trunk – and still be street legal. You are therefore left with an important decision to make – do you adapt your vehicle now or, if you plan to continue to use it on a daily basis, do you make any amendments closer to Z-Day? Alternatively, if you have the budget, you could purchase a second vehicle especially for zombie apocalypse conversion purposes.

THE GOLDEN RULES

If you are "tooling up" your vehicle, there are some golden rules you need to consider before you even start. The first relates to weight and over-loading your vehicle ("weapons platform" in survival speak). The second is about blending in and not standing out. The third relates to getting your hands on whatever firepower you can. If there was a further rule, it would be to practice with your vehicle – only in this way can you iron out any issues with your weaponry.

- Body armor on the wrong vehicle will drastically slow you down. Ensure that you have the right base vehicle and then improve as appropriate. Manage the weight of your vehicle very carefully during any conversion process.
- Don't overlook the benefit of your vehicle blending in. A dirty, bashed up, and non-descript exterior is ideal if you, for example, leave it parked as you go off foraging. Consider therefore whether to fit your M60z now or keep it hidden on the back seat until needed.
- Not easy in the US, but you need to get your hands on some firepower to put raiders off and defend against the dead. Think guns, crossbows, and any ranged weapons, supported by your standard clubbing weapons. You cannot rely on defensive weapons alone – you must be able to project your attacks if required.

▶ ROOF MOUNTED MACHINE GUN

There are many ways to add firepower to your vehicle, with many hardcore preppers preferring two hood mounted machine or rail guns. But if you're new to this and are thinking about converting your family car then a roof mounted option is the best place to start. Your first port of call should be to ensure that you have a sunroof fitted. If you don't, you'll need one. Even if you do, a standard fitted sunroof is not sufficient to mount weapons such as the popular M60z. It is worth getting a professional to create the weapons sub-structure as an unstable platform can render this powerful weapon almost useless. In most configurations, at least one seat is removed from the interior to make space for an integrated ammunition box and belt feed.

"FOR MOST DRIVERS, FIREARMS ARE HARD TO SOURCE AT BEST AND IN MANY CASES ILLEGAL. SURVIVALISTS NEED TO GET CREATIVE. DON'T OVERLOOK THE POTENTIAL OF ITEMS SUCH AS NAIL-GUNS AND FRONTAL SCOOPS."
MICK "FROSTY" HILLS, ZOMBIE SURVIVALIST, EX-SAS TROOPER

▶ REAR-FLAME TAIL GUN

This is where things get toasty and serious. Flame throwing weapons are dangerous to use and deploy but can be devastating against the walking dead. This unit can only be ordered in the US at the moment and isn't cheap – a kit costs around $4,000 plus fitting and a day's training. However, imagine the feeling when you fry up a horde of zombies who are chasing your vehicle or when you scare off a gang of would-be looters with a puff of flame. Not for the faint-hearted, fitting a rear-flame weapon could be invaluable to clear off any pursuing hordes or enemy vehicles but it's a serious investment, plus some experts consider the danger of carrying the flame-fuel on board to be enough of a risk to outweigh the obvious street cred benefits.

"A FLAME WEAPON IS NOT FOR EVERYONE – IT'S A SERIOUS PIECE OF EQUIPMENT AND REQUIRES FITTING BY A SPECIALIST. THERE ARE SO MANY WAYS IT COULD ALL GO WRONG. WIND BLOWS THE FLAME THE WRONG WAY – GAME OVER."
TONY "WINKLE" HODGETTS, FORMER RAC PATROLMAN AND ZOMBIE SURVIVALIST

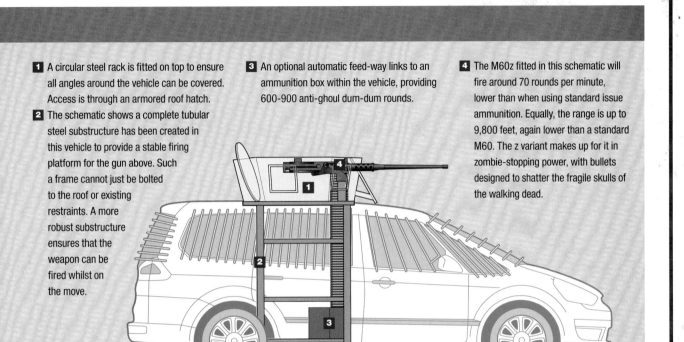

1 A circular steel rack is fitted on top to ensure all angles around the vehicle can be covered. Access is through an armored roof hatch.

2 The schematic shows a complete tubular steel substructure has been created in this vehicle to provide a stable firing platform for the gun above. Such a frame cannot just be bolted to the roof or existing restraints. A more robust substructure ensures that the weapon can be fired whilst on the move.

3 An optional automatic feed-way links to an ammunition box within the vehicle, providing 600-900 anti-ghoul dum-dum rounds.

4 The M60z fitted in this schematic will fire around 70 rounds per minute, lower than when using standard issue ammunition. Equally, the range is up to 9,800 feet, again lower than a standard M60. The z variant makes up for it in zombie-stopping power, with bullets designed to shatter the fragile skulls of the walking dead.

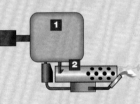

1 Most rear-flame tail guns are fitted with the igniter unit extending from underneath the bumper behind the vehicle to a distance of around 4 inches. This clearance is important for safety reasons.

2 Some models are disguised as down-pointing exhaust pipes and fry up the ground behind the vehicle – these variations have an automatic igniter safety catch which is enabled when the vehicle is stationary.

3 Your flame-fuel reserve is typically inside the trunk, with a controlling unit in the cabin, enabling those inside to switch the weapon on for short bursts of up to 3 seconds.

4 A standard unit with a full flame-fuel load is capable of around 10 such 3 second bursts, sending flames up to 33 feet to the rear of the vehicle.

MOTORIZED TRANSPORT

ON-BOARD WEAPONS —

Storing firearms or any kind of weapon in your vehicle will present challenges. Most obvious of all of course is that your vehicle will not be street legal with a fitted rear-flame thrower and an M60 sticking out of a firing port on the roof. However, there are also guidelines you should follow when keeping weapons in a confined space such as keeping any Bug-Out Weapons in a secure and locked case when not on 'missions', using safety catches where appropriate and ensuring that anyone using a weapon, be it your M60 or a baseball bat with barbed wire and nail accessories, is trained and competent to use it in combat. All sounds like common sense but remember that survival experts estimate that almost 20% of all prepper casualties in any emergency are victims of unintentional wounds inflicted using their own weapons.

▶ DECOMPOSITION FILTER OR "DECOMP KIT"

A specialist piece of anti-zombie kit that can be fitted to virtually any exhaust pipe. A decent "Decomp Kit" will typically cost around $400 but is a very worthwhile investment. It can be fitted with no visible impact and does not affect the emission standards of your vehicle during any MOT testing. Just remember not to leave the dead scent filter on or the garage could end up with some very strange results. Most units come with full instructions and can be fitted without the need for specialist tools. It is worth checking vehicle compatibility online before ordering as most filters won't fit very new cars or heavy goods vehicles.

1 The base unit is fitted to the underside of the vehicle. In most configurations, it is between the catalytic converter and the muffler. (Warning – a decomposition unit is not a replacement for the catalytic converter.)

2 Inside the base unit, there are several cells, each of which contains replaceable chemical pellets. Typically, there are 3 units on each side – the dead pellets and the live pellets.

3 The unit is controlled from within the cabin. Activate the dead cells and your vehicle will leave a trail of "zombie scent" behind it. When stationary, the dead scent fills the air and the dead become disinterested and shamble off.

4 Equally, activate the living cell and the dead will be drawn to you, enabling you to build up a tail of following zombies. Useful for clearing an area or offensive operations against fellow survivors.

CONTROL UNIT

Different makers produce different control units but most have three settings for your filter. "Off" indicates no activity from the unit, exhaust fumes will flow through as per normal. "Dead" activates one of the cells within the unit to release zombie-like dead scent. The "Live" similarly releases a live-flesh scent.

⚠ **IMPORTANT**

ALWAYS TAKE INTO ACCOUNT THAT FUMES IN THE AIR ARE AFFECTED BY ENVIRONMENTAL FACTORS – FOR EXAMPLE, THE FILTERS PERFORM POORLY WHEN MOVING AT SPEED OR IN WINDY CONDITIONS AND ARE VIRTUALLY USELESS IN THE RAIN.

PACK 1
THE ESSENTIALS
STAY STREET LEGAL BUT STILL ZOMBIE RESISTANT

Pack 1 contains key elements familiar to any survivalist or prepper and focuses on keeping your vehicle street legal (just) and will drastically improve your general disaster and zombie preparedness. If you are on a limited budget or restricted to one car then this pack of survival goodies is where you start. Much of it is common sense and will fit discreetly into most cars. It should be supported by a full maintenance schedule for the vehicle and remember to rotate any water and food in your Bug-Out Supplies. Importantly, ensure that you run regular tests with your vehicle. One exercise could be to run through the house at 02.00 am screaming about zombies. Get the rest of the family into the car and practice bugging out by driving 100 miles up the highway. Can your family survive on your Bug-Out supplies alone? Given time, they will certainly appreciate the benefits of your early morning training regime.

- ▶ Fully equipped Bug-Out Trunk Pack
- ▶ Basic tool and spares kit
- ▶ Plastic sheeting and emergency shelter
- ▶ Jerry can of fuel (with rotation plan)
- ▶ Hand pump and siphon
- ▶ Extra clothing pack
- ▶ Emergency food and water (48 hours for 4 people)
- ▶ Basic first aid kit
- ▶ Street legal weapons

PACK 2
ZOMBIE DEFENCE BASICS
FUN ZOMBIE-BUSTING STUFF FOR ALL DRIVERS

This is where things get spicy. Zombies aren't good at getting into cars but there are some basic improvements you can make to make your vehicle a "zombie-killa." Pack 2 vacuum in that grey area between almost legal and "I'm sorry officer I had no idea there was a flame-thrower in my trunk." It includes basics such as having a mesh grill over the windows and mean looking frontal bull bars that are going to get you noticed on the school run. If you're serious about preparing your vehicle for the zombie apocalypse then this is the time to consider buying a second vehicle and turning it into your primary Bug-Out Vehicle. Remember that items such as a razor-sharp cutting scoop and vehicle mounted flare guns will mean your vehicle failing its inspection and will therefore impact on your insurance premiums.

- ▶ Front steel bull bars
- ▶ Additional cage protection bars around the corners and rear
- ▶ Metal mesh protective cover on all windows
- ▶ Floor hatch to provide emergency exit
- ▶ Front-fitted zombie scoop
- ▶ Decomposition filter on the exhaust
- ▶ Rear-Flame Tail Gun (optional)
- ▶ Vehicle mounted flare array

PACK 3
THE ROAD WARRIOR
AND FINALLY, THINGS GET SERIOUS

Pack 3 will transform your vehicle from a zombie defence machine into a set of wheels in which you can dominate the wasteland. It involves major changes where appropriate to accommodate an array of weapons and on-board defences. Most vehicles at this level will be SUVs, pickups, or larger cars but it is possible to convert a smaller passenger car – you will just have to consider the power-weight ratio or you will end up with an under-performing vehicle and a chronic over-heating problem. In this volume, you'll find items such as roof-mounted M60s and rear-vehicle flamers – in fact, there are thousands of variations of weapons you can fit to your Bug-Out Vehicle. Add to this full car body armor and bulletproof glass. Pack 1 prepares you for survival. Pack 2 for the zombies. Pack 3 is not only about defending yourself against the growing threat of human bandits but also about having the kind of vehicle to support a new lifestyle in the wasteland.

- ▶ Vehicle structure strengthening – steel bar support body pack
- ▶ Armalite apocalypse car-body armor (where vehicle allows)
- ▶ Armalite bulletproof glass to all windows
- ▶ Fuel tank booster (armored)
- ▶ On-board firearms cabinet
- ▶ Roof-mounted firearms (optional)
- ▶ Additional storage space (involves seat removal)

MOTORIZED TRANSPORT

THE PERFECT ZOMBIE APOCALYPSE VEHICLE

It's important not to get overwhelmed by the hundreds of Bug-Out or apocalypse vehicles on offer and the countless variations and improvements you can make to boost your survival chances. Think of this manual as a work book, packed with ideas – some of which will work for you, others which won't. Every survivor has a unique plan when it comes to transportation during a zombie apocalypse, and no two Bug-Out systems are the same. Indeed many preppers keep their own plans under wraps for

obvious reasons. However, in the diverse and bizarre world of zombie survival, there are some individuals who do speak out and who freely share information and plans with the general aim of increasing humanity's preparedness for a zombie outbreak.

Crown Prince Hussein Bin Abdullah of Jordon is one such person and has used his own fortune to actively sponsor zombie survival initiatives all over the world.

▶ THE ZOM 90E ROAD WARRIOR (PROTOTYPE)

Nothing is perfect – at least that's what they say – and they may be right but this ghoul-busting prototype car comes pretty close. With currently only 5 in existence, it's going to be hard to get your grubby hands on but it's worth reading the features list alone for the countless innovations and ideas included to help the driver survive and even prosper in a wasteland littered with the walking dead and human bandits. The car comes out of a famous automotive lab in Amman, Jordan, where scientists and engineers from across the region have been working together to create a gold-standard zombie survival vehicle.

"MY WHOLE OBJECTIVE WITH THIS VEHICLE WAS TO CREATE A PROTOTYPE WHICH CAN BE SHOWN TO CAR MANUFACTURERS AROUND THE WORLD. I'VE HAD PROMISING MEETINGS WITH A MAJOR MANUFACTURER ALREADY – MAINLY ABOUT THE POSSIBILITY OF CONVERTING THE ZOM 90E INTO A STREET LEGAL MASS-PRODUCED CAR, WHICH PREPPERS COULD THEN ADD TO AS THE NEED ARISES."
CROWN PRINCE HUSSEIN BIN ABDULLAH

THE ZOM 90E ROAD WARRIOR
Manufactured by the Royal Jordanian Automotive Consortium, currently with 5 versions of the 90E in discussion. Technical plans available on request.

PURPOSE
The ultimate road-warrior vehicle designed to rule the wasteland and be tough enough to fight off both zombies and any human aggressors.

TECHNICAL SPECIFICATIONS
This model is based on a seriously upgraded Hyundai Veloster Turbo. The model is a 4-door hatchback armed with a blistering 1.8 custom bi-fuel compatible TCi GDi engine. The transmission is a 7-speed automatic DCT. Importantly, the team wanted to use a production car as a base for the 90E, with another of the prototypes built on the frame of a Toyota Hilux, and another using an ex-police force Honda CR-V.

ARMAMENTS
These vehicles really pack a punch. The primary weapon is a swivel M60 which is accessed via a roof hatch. The secondary armament consists of twin experimental IWI Negev 7.64mm machine guns mounted on each wing. The twin Negevs can be directed from within the cabin. Additional weapons include a zombie leg slicing chainsaw.

RANGE
The Hyundai variant has a range of around 400 miles, which can be increased by use of an additional internal tank to 500 miles. It achieves up to 30 miles per gallon, which is impressive given its level of armour and weaponry.

CREW
The vehicle can carry 4 survivors, complete with Bug-Out Supplies and weapons but 3 is more comfortable for long-distance travel.

BUDGET
Not released. Experts estimate a budget of around $100,000. Also worth considering is Toyota and Honda variations which reports indicate both come in at under $70,000. (These estimates exclude firearm and ammunition costs.)

USAGE GUIDELINES
The ZOM 90E is a punchy and fast ride ideally suited to navigating the wasteland after the fall of civilization. Its gearing gives it excellent acceleration and the steering is responsive and the car maneuverable. You can defend yourself against most opponents and the all-round armor means that it's possible to carry out ram-raids, making use of the roof or back exit to procure supplies without having to venture outside and face the zombies.

> **"WE DID SET OUT TO BUILD THE BEST ROAD FIGHTING VEHICLE WE COULD. STRONG FRAME, PUNCHY ENGINE, REINFORCED DRIVE MECHANISM, AND ENOUGH FIREPOWER TO START A SMALL WAR."**
> **CROWN PRINCE HUSSEIN BIN ABDULLAH**

FEATURES

- Mottled purple-green anti-zombie non-reflective paint, made using chemical compounds which repel the infected and create an inhospitable environment for the virus in any splattered blood.
- Reinforced darkened bulletproof windows with steel mesh protection. The zombies can't see you so there's always the option go quiet and release the dead scent from the under-vehicle decomposition unit causing any nearby zombies to lose interest.
- External storage racks for two full-sized spares wheels. Tyres are special issue Bridgestone Turanza Z001s.
- Four door access plus roof hatch and rear door emergency exit – ideally configured for rapid exit and entry when out foraging.
- On-board firework, smoke bomb, and grenade launching unit, controlled from a central defensive systems array on the dashboard.
- Light-weight B4 grade ballistic body armor around main body and doors.
- Roof mounted M60z firing head –

smashing low velocity rounds which are also effective against bandits.

- Twin experimental Negev anti-zombie machine guns, firing experimental ghoul-busting dum dum bullets. Both guns are fed from an under-bonnet ammunition box.
- A network of 22 perimeter defence sensors around the vehicle which detect both movement and heat, feeding data back to the central defensive array on the dashboard. Vehicle also includes detachable sensors to establish a perimeter sensor network, for example during periods of sleep.
- Next generation Zombie Whistle Unit which generates noise at an ultrasonic level and is said to repel the dead and newly infected.
- Quad-batteries array on-board with a re-charging handle in the rear of the vehicle. An "eternity" T100 start-up system ensures a minimal charge.
- Fully equipped Bug-Out Trunk including a 5

gallon fresh water tank, plus 5 internal lockable, and 2 hidden compartments. Plus additional door storage unit for 10 military ready-to-eat meals.

- Secure on-board storage for two AK-47zs plus a ceiling holster for shotgun. A concealed handgun holster is under the steering column.
- Two horde clearer chainsaws at the front of the vehicle which move side to side to clear masses of the dead. These saws are retractable during off-road driving. Fully wrapped bull bars and an interior protective screen covering the engine.
- Communications array including a set of 5 2-way short-range "walkie-talkie" units with encryption and military-grade location units. Plus a dashboard mounted CB system and a navigation suite with sealed unit and downloaded maps.

MOTORIZED TRANSPORT

FUEL FOR SURVIVORS

With the right vehicle choice and the right maintenance regime, you should confidently be able to keep your vehicle "on the road" and enjoy many years of happy, post-zombie apocalypse driving. However, the biggest question on most survivalist agendas is about fuel – be it gas or diesel. Will motoring survivalists face dry tanks within weeks or simply a small price hike at local "end of the world" fuel outlets? Also, what about other forms of power? Living in the US, we get enough sun rays per day to power a small matchbox car using solar energy. There are other options – hydrogen fuel cells, steam, coal, even utilizing zombie power – but for most of us, it's going to be a Mad Max-like fuel grab.
So where to nab that precious transport nectar?

HOW MUCH GAS IS THERE IN THE US?

The truth is no one really knows the answer else they just got too bored trying to work it out so here are some factors to consider:

▶ The US national demand for road fuels is 142.98 billion gallons per year.
▶ That equates to around 391 million gallons of road fuels per day.
▶ There are around 114,500 gas stations in the US, virtually all of them with underground storage tanks. Most of them also serve a delightful range of snacks and hot drinks.

▶ THE FUEL LANDSCAPE

In consultation with experts – and we mean real experts – the Ministry of Zombies has put together the following graphic to illustrate the very real fuel challenges every survivor will face. However, you'll see that there are surprising sources of fuel as well – sites perhaps other looters and foragers will miss.

1 REFINERY COMPLEX

A good location to forage for fuel and other supplies in the early days but after a few months expect the site to have been taken over by an ambitious warlord. Only the biggest groups will have the resources to get a plant running and they may also start selling off fuel from any on-site storage tanks.

2 GAS STATIONS

An obvious location which will become a hotbed of looting from day one – with the on-site shop being a clear target for supplies. Depending on the speed of the crisis, some stations will already be dry, with lines of empty and abandoned vehicles blocking the way.

3 FACTORIES AND DEPOTS

Many industrial and distribution sites have on-site fuel storage facilities. Post offices and anyone operating a delivery network are likely to provide particularly rich pickings for fuel foraging as well as good sites for spares and extras. Many of these sites will be overlooked during the initial fuel panic so get in early and grab what you can.

4 AIRPORTS

Every zombie survivalist knows to stay away from airports in the opening weeks of the crisis but as time goes on, they can provide useful sources of fuel supplies. Whilst aviation fuel is largely useless apart from use in a car-mounted flame thrower, it's the network of car parks which could provide the best areas for foraging.

5 CENTERS OF AUTHORITY

Remember, only forage from any emergency sites if you are sure that they are abandoned. Be sure that you don't interrupt any vital work against the zombies. However, if you do find any police, fire stations or other government sites, it's well worth a look around.

6 CAR SHOWROOMS AND GARAGES

Useful if you fancy grabbing a new vehicle for the apocalypse. Fuel storage on site is not typically very significant but there is usually a tank somewhere and any used cars outside would be worth checking out. Garages are likely to provide a similar haul in terms of fuel but are perfect locations for spares and consumables.

7 HOME SUPPLIES

Most homes will yield little in the way of fuel supplies bar the family car on the drive. If you happen to stumble on a well-prepared zombie prepper then you can expect them to be ready for any would-be looters. It may be possible to trade with them for fuel.

8 OTHER VEHICLES

Trawling the streets, looking for untouched cars will become a staple activity for many survivors hunting for fuel. It's important that you get your siphoning kit and skills ready to go and it's worth stocking up on some decent cans to support your activities. You can expect fuel from cars in the street to become scarce very quickly.

▶ The immediate days after the breakdown of civilization will see many of these locations looted, plundered, and even burnt, particularly in urban areas. Quadruple the normal lines at gas stations and throw in several hundred ravenous zombies.

▶ Official sources calculate that there are about 268 million vehicles on our roads. That includes passanger cars, trucks, buses, and other vehicles. That's a lot of wheels. So, if you have the kit, there is plenty of fuel out there in tanks but it won't last forever.

▶ The whole fuel system is supported by a nationwide network of pipelines which move millions of tons of fuel around the US, with road and rail transport being responsible for movement to end locations.

So what does it all mean? It means things are going to get frosty around any type of fuel. If you are a serious zombie prepper you can experiment with alternative power sources such as ethanol but, for most, this makes it even more important that you factor in fuel security into your Bug-Out Plans. There is plenty of information out there on other power options such as steam and even nuclear energy but, for the moment, you have to accept we live in a fossil fuel world.

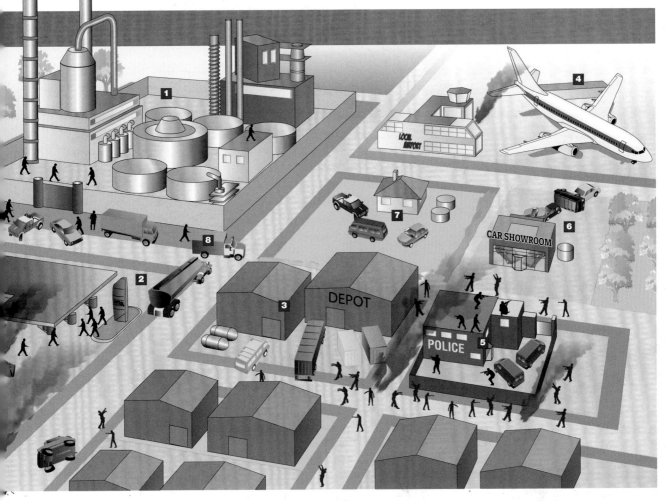

THE POST-APOCALYPTIC GARAGE

Whatever your Bug-Out Vehicle of choice, you will need a secure and well-equipped base from which to operate and maintain it. If you're planning on a long-range Bug-Out journey then it could be as simple as a location to keep your vehicle safe until it's needed. For example, you'll want to ensure it's safe from any prying eyes before the dead rise and that opportunistic bandits can't help themselves to it once the chaos begins. Equally, if you are planning to use your fortified home as a base from which to forage and expand – then you'll need a secure workshop, fully equipped with spares, fuel and everything necessary to keep you on the road. Don't underestimate the challenge of building this vital workspace; it's just as important as your vehicle. In the new world, there won't be organised garages or the RAC. You might find some useful stores from which to forage supplies but in terms of maintenance and keeping mobile – you'll be on your own.

▶ END OF THE WORLD GARAGE

A fortified garage area is essential to keep you on the road after the end of the world. Like many survival projects, you can start small, for example by reinforcing the front doors and meshing the windows. Create a plan for any work and make a rule to spend at least a day every week in your garage, either working on your vehicle, studying survival manuals or brushing up your mechanical skills. Ideally, the workshop should be within easy reach of your home complex or at least have a secure route to your vehicle and supplies. The End of the World Garage in this case study in based on a real-life survivor example in Birmingham. The plans show the core elements of the workshop but in reality, the owner has gone to significant lengths to ensure the site looks more like an abandoned lock up than a fully equipped workshop. For example, she secured a burnt-out wreck from a breakers yard which now sits on the drive. The roof and steel fence is largely covered by ivy, with a rotting sofa blocking the door. At first glance, any would-be looters would just assume that it is some crumbling old building. "No one outside the immediate family knows what I've built here," she explains. "Every bit has been smuggled in, mostly at night. Advertise your end of the world garage and it will be the first thing to go once the riots start."

1 LOCATION IS KEY
You must have easy access from your fortified home – the last thing you want is to be cut off from your vehicles in an emergency.

2 THE MAIN DOOR
If you have an old-fashioned up and over garage door, make it the first thing that you change. These older doors cave in with the least bit of pressure. Replace it with reinforced steel rollers or something similar.

3 SURVIVAL LIBRARY
Keep a stock of survival books, including a Haynes manual of your particular vehicle. There will be long periods of inactivity during the crisis so use this time to top up your know-how.

4 TRAINING CERTIFICATES
Proudly display your mechanic and engineering qualifications. Track your achievements and learn everything you can about maintaining your vehicle.

5 EXTERIOR DEFENCES
A 6-foot reinforced steel fence is ideal but can stick out in an urban landscape. Razor wire can have much the same effect. A secure outside space is important so use items such as burnout cars or other debris to conceal your fortifications. If fencing is going to be too obvious then just go for fortified doors.

⚠ IMPORTANT

THERE ARE ALL TYPES OF HEALTH AND SAFETY CONCERNS AROUND THE STORAGE OF FUEL. AS A GENERAL GUIDELINE, GAS IN A PURPOSE-BUILT SEALED CONTAINER SUCH AS A CAN WILL LAST 3–6 MONTHS BUT IF YOU ADD FUEL STABILIZER, YOU CAN ADD ANOTHER 2–3 MONTHS ON TOP OF THIS. DIESEL FUEL CAN BE STORED FOR AROUND A YEAR WITH LITTLE DEGRADATION BUT IF YOU GET THE RIGHT CONDITIONS, IT CAN LAST A LOT LONGER.

6 FUEL STORAGE

Ensure that you have a suitable and safe fuel storage area. Remember to date any fuels so you can rotate your stocks.

7 SPARES AND STORAGE

Maintain an ample supply of spare parts and consumables. Check vehicle breaker yards for extra parts but order other parts such as batteries new.

8 TOOL CABINET

Maintain your stock and tools to ensure you can maintain your vehicle and home.

9 SOUND AND LIGHT PROOFING

This can be an expensive alteration but getting your location sound and light proofed will ensure that you can operate safely at all times while still running to the outside world. No other survivors will be aware of any work you are doing inside and, importantly, your constant banging or Little Mix compilation won't attract the unwelcome attention of the walking dead.

10 A SECURE BOLTHOLE

Many zombie survival planners build concealed boltholes within their structures. This could be a hidden cupboard or trapdoor to a small fortified space you can hide in if the need arises. Ensure you have some basic supplies and water inside. If raiders or zombies get in and you can't defeat them, hiding could be your only option to survive.

REMEMBER

Always disguise your End of the World Garage. Keep your activities secret and ensure that the site looks like any normal garage. A careless boast could make your site a target for raiders.

ZOMBIE APOCALYPSE RV

Campervans or RVs are superb Bug-Out Vehicles but getting a good rig is not cheap and even the best non-purpose RVs need some adaptions to ensure they are zombie-safe. For example, most regular RVs have extremely thin fibreglass or plastic walls – these certainly need strengthening. As a general guideline, it's better to buy than rent and be prepared for some high gas bills as you practice your zombie outbreak evacuation plans. Go for the best machine you can afford – if necessary spend more on a robust frame then add homemade zombie defences. A great strength of RVs and similar vehicles is that you can pretty much carry everything with you. Also, if you have the right supplies, you hardly need to stop, therefore greatly reducing your chances of running into the walking dead. One thing to remember though is to watch the weight of your vehicle, particularly when you start factoring in supplies attached to the roof, any armor or shielding and additional fuel tanks.

You can also look at converting light commercial or heavy goods vehicles into RV-type configurations by building in living spaces and defences.

▶ MULTICAT ZOMBIECROSS 60 "THE WINCHESTER"

The perfect Mad Max-style post-apocalyptic cruiser is ideal if you're travelling solo, or plan to rule the zombie wasteland as a mysterious street warrior, but what if you're stuck in a 3-bedroom semi, have 2.4 kids and a 9–5 office job? How can you get your travel needs sorted short of soldering armor plates to the aging people carrier you use for the school run? Well, the answer is the Multicat Zombiecross 60 series – an all-terrain purpose-built family survival vehicle. Before you imagine a camouflage expedition vehicle which is going to stick out in suburbia, this series is designed to look just like a regular recreational vehicle or RV. Read on but be prepared to dig out those forms about taking a second mortgage because this kind of zombie stopping power doesn't come cheap!

"OUR DAUGHTER AMELIA HAS BECOME QUITE THE EXPERT WITH ALL THE ON-BOARD ZOMBIE DEFENCES SUCH AS MANAGING THE MOVEMENT DETECTION SENSOR ARRAYS."
MR MASON, END OF DAYS CARAVANS

THE MASON FAMILY ZOMBIE SURVIVAL PLAN
End of Days (EoD) Caravans, Tampa, Florida

LOCATION
Mr Mason (location withheld). EoD has a showroom in Tampa Bay, Florida, with over 25 models on display.

PURPOSE
"This is our family's apocalypse survival plan. We went for the zombie variation as we thought this was the most likely cause of the end of the world. But, whatever it is – zombies, aliens, the collapse of the economy – this vehicle is going to get us to our Bug-Out Location deep in the New Forest. We've owned it for about 3 years now and have used it every year for holidays both here and abroad."

TECHNICAL SPECIFICATIONS
6 quart, 6-cylinder diesel engine, 320 horsepower and 9-speed manual transmission. All-wheel drive with central lock differential. Sealed anti-ghoul drum brakes. 365/80 R 45 Michelin Zomb-XL tubeless tires. Dimensions – length 25 feet, width 8 feet, height 10 feet. Fully-laden weight 8,800 lbs.

ARMAMENTS
None as standard but military packs can be ordered where it is legal to do so in your country. This version is fitted with a range of anti-zombie features. EoD Caravans reports that one owner in Texas has fitted twin M60s to their machine plus a quick-fire anti-tank weapon.

RANGE
With double 158 gallon fuel tanks, 600–800 miles depending on road conditions. Maximum speed of around 75 mph.

CREW
4–8 persons – can accommodate 12 plus supplies but not in any comfort and this would include several survivors riding shotgun on the roof. Most models can also be fitted with a specially designed Bug-Out Supplies trailer.

BUDGET
$110,000 for the standard version of the Multicat Zombiecross 60 – "The Winchester." Weapons packs come in at around $13,000 each including 4 AK-47z with ammunition boxes. EoD Caravans don't make budget models so all of the components meet military-grade specifications.

USAGE GUIDELINES

Each vehicle is sold as a standard motor home and can be enjoyed on regular holidays. All of the key apocalypse components are hidden from prying eyes. Each vehicle comes with a Zombie Apocalypse Kit (Z-poc Kit) – consisting of the steel bull bars to protect the front of the vehicle plus around a dozen other anti-zombie and raider fortifications. This is so that "The Winchester" can be easily converted once things start getting toasty.

FEATURES

- ▶ Robust 9-speed manual all-terrain transmission with military-grade sealed gearbox and long-life oil filtering system
- ▶ Purpose designed anti-ghoul braking system, calibrated to clear up to 1 gallon of zombie gunk per mile
- ▶ Hardened R 45 Michelin Zomb-XL tyres – tough enough to handle any road conditions. Wheels also include a patented coded quick release mechanism
- ▶ 26 storage compartments across the vehicle including 10 lockable and 3 hidden storage spaces

- ▶ Movement sensors around the vehicles
- ▶ Triple smoke launchers
- ▶ Fully tinted, toughened glass windows
- ▶ Self-supporting UNICAT sandwich plate panels of fortified zombie-proof fibreglass composite
- ▶ Under body emergency escape hatch
- ▶ Top hatch and light machine gun firing port
- ▶ Extended emergency fuel tank
- ▶ Seating area for 4–6 persons, with adjustable swivelling table on pedestal in the front of the cabin
- ▶ Seating unit converts to additional double bed
- ▶ Combined sealed shower and toilet room with door to isolate from living area
- ▶ Oven with microwave and deep apocalypse-class 40-gallon fridge
- ▶ Overhead cupboards above kitchen units and emergency food rations
- ▶ LPG 4-flame stove
- ▶ 211 gallon freeze-proof drinking water tanks

- ▶ Waste water tank – capacity 46 gallons
- ▶ Diesel powered warm water central heating (7 kW)
- ▶ High radiant heat share due to radiators in living area, sanitary room and bed area
- ▶ Bicycle carrier at rear
- ▶ Spare wheel carrier at the rear and on the roof
- ▶ Off the grid 1000E washing machine
- ▶ Water filtration system
- ▶ Roof slots and floor restraints to enable an additional storage unit or firing platform to be fitted to the roof and which can be accessed by either a ladder at the rear or an optional internal roof hatch.

MOTORIZED TRANSPORT

ZOMBIE BATTLE BUS

There is significant interest in the zombie prepping community around converting vehicles into "battle buses" – that is long-range, armored and armed moving bases, which can cope with both zombies and the dangerous conditions in the wasteland. Here we profile a London Routemaster bus conversion.

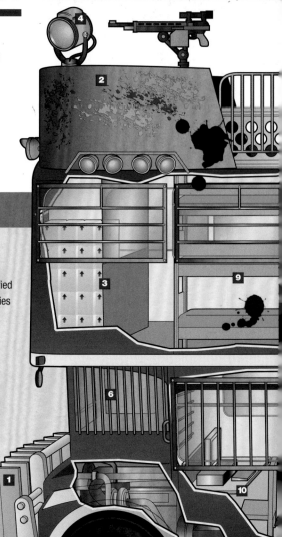

▶ THE ROUTEMASTER APOCALYPSE BUS

Iconic and instantly recognisable, many will be surprised to learn that the original designers of the famous Routemaster bus in the late 1940s had always planned a post-apocalyptic version. Unfortunately, only fragmentary plans exist for their Cold War "Battle Bus" but models assembled before 1978 were indeed built on a military-grade chassis, providing a vehicle strength far beyond what is normal.

THE ROUTEMASTER APOCALYPSE BUS
Mrs Wakely, Boggy Bottom, Hertfordshire

LOCATION
Hidden in a local barn, safe from prying village nose-poker-inners.

PURPOSE
Long-range post-apocalyptic transporter and live-in bastion

TECHNICAL SPECIFICATIONS
1965 RM2120 Routemaster (restored), original front suspension, power steering and automatic gearbox. 1972 Leyland 10 litre Supra-Diesel Engine. All aluminium stressed skin construction. Complete interior rebuild.

ARMAMENTS
2 hand guns from World War 1, 1 fowling piece, Grandad's shotgun and a set of vintage golf clubs.

RANGE
The standard capacity on a Routemaster is around 34 gallons – this model has a modified tank with a capacity of 53 gallons plus carries a full set of 5-gallon safety gas cans. With modifications made to the engine, it can do 7 miles to the gallon so without using emergency supplies and at a steady speed of 30 mph, it can do just over 300 miles.

CREW
"We've built it for the family plus a few neighbors. That's a crew of 12–14."

BUDGET
"Our model was in particularly good condition and we paid $92,000 for her. There are cheaper vehicles out there. If you plan to convert it, ensure that it's a pre-1977 model."

USAGE GUIDELINES
'We plan to use our bus as a Bug-Out Vehicle. We've found a secluded beach in Devon which will be easy to seal off from the zombies. We plan to head there then use the bus as our home. We increased our fuel tank size and spent a tidy sum on it. Luckily, I had a bingo win so spent the cash on getting a specialist in to complete the work. Always go for the older models as they are easier to maintain."

FEATURES
1 A reinforced steel front scoop, built to clear any obstruction, be it broken down cars or zombie hordes. The scoop is detachable and can be stored on the roof, which improves the vehicles off-road performance.

2 Front and rear integrated armoured weapons stations, both shown with a modified FN Herstal light machine gun, with 100 round disintegrating belts.

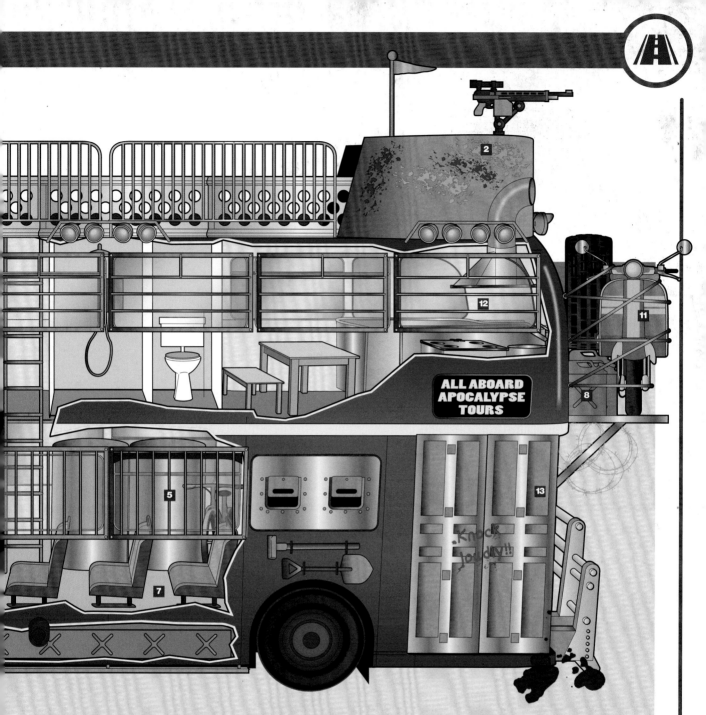

ALL ABOARD APOCALYPSE TOURS

3 Main Bug-Out supplies in air-cooled storage. As a general guide, there is enough for 1–2 months of supplies for a party of 10–14 survivors. Fresh food is stored in under-floor tanks in different sections of the vehicle.

4 A directional spotter lamp with integrated infra-red and "Zombie Cool-Vision" camera.

5 Two vast 26-gallon armored fuel tanks, enabling a fully-laden vehicle to complete around 300 miles without refuelling.

6 Fortified driver station, with meshed windows all-around, plus access to 6 internal and external CCTV cameras.

7 Travel seating for 8 survivors, with under-seat storage.

8 Emergency external fuel reserves and spare wheel tool station, everything required to keep the bus on the road.

9 6-berth sleeping cabin – typically used as 'hotbeds' for survivors.

10 Map and navigation system, with a shielded computer monitoring system of on-board systems.

11 50cc Honda moped, used for foraging.

12 Kitchen and canteen area with full specification refrigerator unit, quad-hob, oven and storage.

13 Fortified steel concertina folding doors, with viewing port. Alternative exits include a floor hatch to escape under the vehicle.

MOTORCYCLE OPTIONS

"Two wheels good, four wheels bad" is not something author George Orwell said, but had he known his motorbikes and some elements of basic zombie survival, he might well have.

Two wheeled and smaller vehicles such as quad bikes and dune buggies have some real advantages over larger options as they can weave through a landscape littered with broken vehicles and obstructions. They also have superb fuel economy – some specialist survival machines boast over 100 miles to the gallon.

There's plenty of choice out there. Obviously, budget is going to be a consideration – after all, not everyone has $33,000 for a custom-built American zombie apocalypse chopper. Could you make the same impact on raiders riding a jazzed-up Honda 50 moped complete with practical front shopping basket? Maybe not.

KNOW YOUR MACHINE

Checking your motorbike over is even more important than ever. Any breakdown in zombie land could prove fatal so remember all the basics – fuel, tires, etc. Have a light-weight Bug-Out Bag on your vehicle at all times, even if it's stuffed in the bottom of a pannier. Importantly, have a good understanding of your machine's ability – if it's a smart road cruiser don't get caught trying to ride over a major obstruction – know, for example, your ground clearance levels.

Most experts predict that poor training and poor knowledge of their bike will get more riders killed during a zombie outbreak than anything else.

OPTION 1
MINI-BIKES

Not the children's models, the fully working versions often used by people dropping off hire cars. Some models can fold and fit in the back of a car. Fast enough to get you out of trouble when required and yet small enough to be part of an on-board Bug-Out Kit on a larger vehicle. The low-profile makes the rider hard to spot but range is limited, particularly on the electric versions. Not great stability wise and suffers from naturally low ground clearance. The gas versions tend to be noisy and attract the zombies but are better performers speed-wise. It might be worth snagging a couple and keeping them in the back of your Bug-Out Garage.

 Poor. The lower you are, the more likely you are to get grabbed. Might be a useful addition if you have ample storage space on your vehicle. But still, only use in real emergencies.

OPTION 2
MOPEDS/SCOOTERS

From mods to grannies, mopeds and scooters are everywhere so availability of these machines is excellent. Basic models are easy to maintain and there are plenty of spare parts out there. 50cc mopeds tend to have a maximum speed of around 40 mph but some larger-engine scooters are faster. A low centre of gravity increases your chances of a crash on obstructed roads. Plus, you will look a bit of an old fart given the choice of other vehicles available, unless you manage to pick up a Quadrophenia-type 250cc super-scooter – more likely you'll end up on a former pizza-delivery moped struggling up hills, weighed down with foraged supplies.

 Good. A basic moped could be a useful back-up option but it's not for a primary vehicle. If you have the budget, it's worth nabbing a cheap second-hand moped and keeping safe.

OPTION 3
ROAD CRUISER

Powerful and extremely quick, these machines are built for performance and speed. To be fair, it's a broad category covering everything from street-legal racing machines to long-distance cruisers, the latter of which can be a useful long-range Bug-Out options, particularly machines such as the Honda Gold Wing series and many of the BMW hybrid cruisers. Generally very good fuel economy and outstanding reliability. The racing machines are great on perfect roads but post-zombie apocalypse roads won't be perfect. They also have 'steal me' written all over it. New machines require specialist technical maintenance and tools.

 Racing machines are not ideal as the road conditions won't suit your sparkling new mean machine. Hybrid road cruisers with greater off-road capability are a better choice.

KNOW YOURSELF

Expert riders always say "ride within your capabilities." Sensible advice for normal times, but in the chaos of the apocalypse it's even more important. Even a minor accident could get you eaten. Training is key – get as much riding training as you can before the dead rise.

LOOKING AHEAD

Target or destination fixation can tempt even experienced riders to focus in the distance when they should be focusing on the road in front. Keep your attention on the road ahead and on any obstructions – that awkwardly parked car or group of desperate survivors hastily putting together an ambush.

PRACTICE DEFENSIVE RIDING

The danger of hostile human drivers is ever-present. Some will see you as a tempting prospect, hoping to knock you off then help themselves to whatever loot you are carrying. Learn how to ride defensively. Use your maneuverability and speed.

OPTION 4
OFF-ROAD BIKES

Perfect for scrambling around roadblocks or across country, these hard-wearing machines are widely available, with many off-road scramblers coming stripped of any non-essential extras. Ensure that you get a reasonable engine size to ensure you have the power and you'll have an excellent machine for the wasteland, capable of clearing most obstacles. The main downside is the noise, with many competition machines barely meeting legal standards so ensure that you check any bike before you buy it as part of your Bug-Out plans. There's a healthy used vehicle market and with common models, spares shouldn't be an issue.

 Very Good. A great short-range Bug-Out vehicle or for foraging. Just get plenty of riding practice before the dead arrive.

OPTION 5
TRIKES

Like off-road bikes, trikes are a great short-range Bug-Out Vehicle and are also good for foraging. Just get plenty of riding practice in before the dead arrive. It's worth fitting some light panniers as storage options aren't great. At reasonable speeds, stability and maneuverability tends to be good but riders need to be familiar with trikes, as there are important differences between 3-wheelers and cars or other motorcycles, particularly the cornering and stability. Advantages are that you can carry passengers and loot. The downsides are that you lack protective cover and the off-road capability of a decent 2-wheeler.

 Good. You'll be a king of the road but will lose the benefits of a 2-wheeled motorcycle and pick up some of the drawbacks of a larger car-like vehicle.

OPTION 6
ATV/QUADS

The stability of a car with the agility of a bike – what's not to love? Good speed and great off-road capability, and with useful people and load carrying options. This broad range of vehicles is a staple feature at most survivalist conventions, from purpose-built "end of the world" quads to 6-wheel all-terrain amphibious "ducks." On most vehicles, the rider is exposed and quad bikes are often more powerful than new riders realise, so it's worth getting some practice in before the apocalypse. Stick to the better known and most common models then adapt from there. Specialist zombie machines tend to be expensive and have to be imported.

 Excellent. As a primary or back-up vehicle, a solid and practical choice for the apocalypse. Any good Honda, Yamaha, or Bombardier model should be a sound platform to build on.

MOTORCYCLE OPTIONS

ZOMBIES AND MOTORCYCLES

There are many dangers out there for motorcyclists in the zombie wasteland. One is that a shambling zombie, attracted by either the noise or movement of your bike, strays into your path. Zombie in the road – bash – you're on the ground getting feasted upon by the rest of the horde. The second danger is grabbers. Be it from the ground or car window, this is a risk for any rider. As one zombie survival rider put it: "I knew a rider who was caught by a zombie from a car window. The thing stuck its hand out and just held on. The rider carried on and the arm just tore off. The thing kept clawing and in the end the guy panicked and rode into a parked car."

If you are planning to use a motorcycle as part of your survival plans beyond just scrambling around on a stripped down off-roader, then you need a powerful, heavy-weight machine, with a low center of gravity and enough on-board storage to carry at least 48 hours of supplies. There are specialist machines available on the market – the Liberty Freedom Wasteland Chopper is one such bike – but they can be beyond the budget of many preppers. Remember that it's quite possible to convert a standard machine by making some alterations. Look through the features on the Liberty Freedom Chopper for some ideas.

▶ LIBERTY 'FREEDOM' WASTELAND CHOPPER

Fantastic fuel economy, cooler than a freezer at Iceland and nothing says "cool" like the Libert "Freedom" Wasteland Chopper – being able to scare opponents could just help you stay alive in zombie town. But this no normal motorcycle, the Freedom Chopper was created by a team of specialist mechanics and zombie survival experts and boasts a host of features to help you rule the wasteland. Available in the "standard" tourer version, there is also a massive range of extras, such as supplementary fuel storage, crossbow holders and smart-code start up. The company slogan is "No one messes with a Freedom Chopper."

"THE TENNESSEE MOTORCYCLE COMPANY SET OUT TO BUILD THE BEST APOCALYPSE-READY MOTORCYCLE WE COULD. WE WANTED TO BUILD THE KIND OF BIKE THAT WOULD GET A SURVIVOR AND PARTNER TO THEIR BUG-OUT LOCATION AT THE END OF THE WORLD."
TENNESSEE MOTORCYCLE COMPANY

THE LIBERTY "FREEDOM" WASTELAND CHOPPER
Tennessee Motorcycle Company, 400 units sold worldwide in 2017

PURPOSE
The ultimate wasteland tourer. See the world solo or with a dream partner and look bad enough to put any opponents off.

TECHNICAL SPECIFICATIONS
Ultima 2.0 dual-fuel engine, liquid cooled. 6-speed transmission with a monocoque aluminium frame. Front suspension Marzocchi 50 mm pressurized forks in hard anodised aluminium. Rear fully adjustable Sachs unit. Front brakes 2,340 mm semi-floating zombie-shielded discs. Rear brakes single 250 mm sealed disc. Front tire 120/70 ZombieR Pirelli Devil. Rear tire 200/55 ZombieR Pirelli Demon.

ARMAMENTS
Optional fittings for handguns, grenade pouches, and semi-automatics. As one owner explained – "This is a chopper screaming to be 'tooled up'."

CREW
1 plus 1 pillion. Survival panniers are included as standard.

BUDGET
The standard tourer version starts at $33,000. There are custom build options; a brochure is available on request. Options include booster panniers, shotgun pouch, and a cleverly shaped extra drinking water tank.

RANGE
300 miles on a standard configuration tank. With the supplementary fuel reserve, can manage 400–500 miles. The multi-fuel engine boasts up to 80 miles to the gallon.

USAGE GUIDELINES
This purpose-built zombie apocalypse chopper is superb wasteland cruiser, with more than enough anti-ghoul features to see you through the outbreak. Ideal as an urban raider for exploring or foraging and with its supplementary fuel tank, can also serve as longer-range Bug-Out Vehicle. Keep out of sight for the first month or so, and then emerge from the garage, complete with your crossbow and survival poncho.

FEATURES

▶ Military grade – uses military-grade parts across the engine including self-cleaning cooling fans and anti-block feed pipes and pumps – basically, zombie guts and gunk aren't going to stop the Wasteland Chopper.

▶ Modern metals – wide use of aluminium across the machine so it so only weighs 250 lbs unladen. Light enough to be controllable but with enough mass to punch through zombie hordes if required. Open optional front screen is available.

▶ Survival Panniers – lockable stowage compartment with in-built water and fuel filtration units, room for two 48 hour Bug-Out Bags and an armored ammunition box. Hidden unit underneath to keep an emergency key.

▶ On-board Weapon Holsters – optional fitting for 'easy access' shotgun storage unit with optional parts to fit weapons such as the Kel-Tec-KSG or longer weapons such as the Remington Model 887. A clever rear catch is designed to hold either a bow or crossbow. There is also additional concealed storage for a small handgun.

▶ Additional Motorcycle Backpack – a hardwearing reinforced canvas sack which fits to the rear of the bike and can be used to store sheeting, tents or other Bug-Out Supplies.

▶ Good ground clearance – a small compromise in the chopper design has lead to slightly shorter front forks and a larger than normal front-wheel to ensure the machine has suitable ground clearance to traverse the wasteland.

▶ Ultima Engine – powerful enough to get you out of any trouble but light enough to give the chopper near-perfect balance – this motor is perfectly suited to the ravages of the wasteland, with a robust filtration system, plus it will run on just about anything.

▶ ZombieR Pirelli Tyres – these bad boys are made for the end times, almost impossible to puncture, military-grade rubberised compound and unique anti-zombie gunk tread.

▶ Gunk proof brake unit – both the front semi-floating discs and the rear single-disc brakes operate as sealed units.

ADVICE ON HELMETS

Protecting your melon when riding or driving any open vehicle during a zombie outbreak is as important as it is now, if not more so. Riders have heard the arguments before:

▶ A quality crash helmet can seriously reduce the risk of head injury and death during an accident

▶ A helmet will also protect you against zombie bites – 21% of zombie bites are to the head and neck area.

▶ It will also protect you from small projectiles hurled by opportunistic survivors looking for easy loot.

IMPORTANT
Always wear a helmet when riding a motorcycle. The benefits far outweigh the disadvantages.

POST-APOCALYPTIC DRIVING

This section outlines the skills you need to develop to survive not only Z-Day but also the growing chaos and violence of the post-apocalyptic world it leaves behind. After all, zombies aren't the only menace you're going to face out there on the roads.

Whatever your vehicle, it is important that you quickly adapt to driving or riding in a post-apocalyptic landscape. A couple of obvious examples will be dealing with various obstructions that will increasingly dominate our roads or the thousands of zombies milling around. However, also consider the new dangers of night-driving on unlit roads and the ever-present threat of human opponents – bandits or even just desperate survivors looking to run you off the road and help themselves to your kit. Training to drive in true zombie apocalypse conditions is impossible. You can, for example, complete various off-road and defensive

driving courses and there is no doubt that these will help but nothing can prepare you for the full horror of an M25 littered with burning lorries, over-turned cars, trapped survivors and the walking dead scouring the landscape for those left alive. This section is all about surviving on post-apocalyptic roads and will provide you with a survival framework including facts, considerations and some basic maneuvers. Nothing can replace real-life practice though so get as much training as you can and practice some of these techniques in controlled conditions.

POST-APOCALYPTIC DRIVING
DRIVER AWARENESS

Working with the Department for Transport, the Ministry of Zombies has created a training framework for driving awareness in conditions affected by a major zombie outbreak. It is hoped that from 2020, elements from this syllabus will be included in the driving theory test, with a focus on zombie hazard perception. In the practical test there will be added elements such as controlling a vehicle with a "screen blocker," where a zombie is clutching onto the windscreen wipers blocking the view – the maneuver is similar to an emergency stop.

> *** THE DEPARTMENT FOR TRANSPORT REQUESTED THAT THE FOLLOWING DISCLAIMER BE MADE**
>
> *The Department for Transport does not endorse Module 3 of the Zombie Apocalypse Driver Awareness program. It is not an objective of this government department to turn leaner or experienced drivers into "Mad Max-style road warriors." It is therefore unlikely that "pulling a U-turn" or "clipping the dead" will included in the driving test any time in the near-future.*

MODULE 1
CONTEXT & ENVIRONMENT

This module involves drivers learning about the general features of post-apocalyptic driving including understanding threats, getting the right driver mentality for the conditions and vehicle preparation.

MODULE 2
ZOMBIE AWARENESS

This module looks at the zombie threat to vehicular transport and drivers, including not only defensive driving techniques but also tried and trusted maneuvers to deal with the zombie menace.

MODULE 3
HOSTILE HUMANS

This controversial module focuses on the human impact of the zombie apocalypse. It considers the "dark skills" required to survive on post-zombie apocalypse streets dominated by desperate survivors and bandits.

▶ CREATE A BUG-OUT ZONE

Consider your secure location in the context of your "Bug-Out Zone" – that is the immediate area around your home and how it supports your survival and Bug-Out Plans. For example, you'll certainly need a good map, marking Bug-Out Routes and other secure locations for use in emergencies. This diagram shows the ideal – most preppers can't afford to have a fully-equipped alternative Bug-Out Vehicle in a fortified lock up but do carefully assess your current location. The principles apply whether you live in a detached or terraced home, or even an apartment.

← RIVER ESCAPE ROUTE

HIDDEN CANOES

5

4 BUG-OUT ROUTE

FORTIFIED HOME

2

1

SURVIVAL CHOPPER

SECURE ALTERNATIVE LOCATION

3

VEHICLE FOR LONG RANGE TRAVEL

CONVERTED FAMILY CAR

1 Your primary Bug-Out Vehicle currently locked in a secure garage but ready to go complete with fuel and Bug-Out Supplies. This is the vehicle that hopefully sees you through the end of the world. You've prepared it, looked after it and now it's ready to face the zombie hordes.

2 There's a survival chopper motorcycle hidden in the garden. It's only a short-range machine but it's intended for foraging around the local area. If the roads are blocked or you don't want to risk your primary vehicle, this is what you use to survey the ruins of civilisation.

3 Your secondary Bug-Out Vehicle is nearby. In this case, it's an old diesel you've maintained and restored, ideal for longer-range journeys. It's stored in the house of a neighbour who lives abroad. People rarely visit the house and only you and your immediate party know about it. Keep it that way!

4 A concealed Bug-Out Route through the nearby woods to the river. It's not a main Bug-Out Route. It's not marked on any of your maps, which could be stolen. This is your emergency path down to the riverside. If zombies or bandits overrun the street and if the roads are completely blocked, this will be your lifeline.

5 Hidden by the river, under a shrub bush, are a couple of canoes, complete with waterproof Bug-Out Bags. You can't see them from the river or the roadside. These waterborne Bug-Out Vehicles are your insurance policy. If things get toasty, you'll head towards these canoes and silently paddle away from the danger.

"DON'T BECOME OBSESSED WITH CREATING THE PERFECT BUG-OUT PLAN. NOT EVERYONE WILL HAVE THE BUDGET FOR MULTIPLE LAYERS OF ESCAPE VEHICLE. START SIMPLE AND LOOK FOR COST-EFFECTIVE AND PRACTICAL OPTIONS. GET YOUR PRIMARY AND SECONDARY VEHICLE SORTED. AFTER THAT, DEVELOP YOUR SYSTEM AS YOU DEVELOP YOUR SKILLS OR HAVE THE BUDGET TO DO SO."
JULIAN HENDRY,
SKILLS FOR THE END OF THE WORLD

POST-APOCALYPTIC DRIVING

CONTEXT AND ENVIRONMENT

If you've done your car or motorcycle driving test then you will often have heard fellow drivers say things like, "It's different on the test, it's not like real life" and, "You really start learning once you've passed." This is true enough and it's the same for the driving conditions after a major zombie outbreak. Being aware of your environment and understanding your vehicle will be vital skills needed to keep you and your group alive.

THREATS ON THE ROAD AFTER Z-DAY

The chart below should guide your transport plans for the apocalypse. For example, it's clear that crashes and collisions kill as many drivers as the zombies do. Also, the figures show the very real threat of human action such as theft and banditry. It's essential that you understand just how much the driving landscape has changed. Remember, these figures relate to the opening few weeks of an outbreak. None of these incidents lasted longer than a month and after this period the number of vehicle breakdowns will increase.

THE C.R.A.Z. SYSTEM

For longer-term predictions, the Ministry of Zombies uses the following **C.R.A.Z** system.

30%	**C**ollision
20%	**R**oad War
30%	**A**uto-breakdown
20%	**Z**ombie Incident

The C.R.A.Z tool is used in all zombie defence planning and offers an aggregated prediction model which estimates transportation casualties during an ongoing zombie apocalypse. So, what it's saying is that of course you need to learn about zombies but collisions, breakdowns and road war incidents will take out far more drivers than the walking dead. This fact has been used to ensure that any military and emergency personnel are as confident in their vehicle and their driving skills as they are at running down the walking dead.

POST-APOCALYPTIC DRIVING
DRIVER DEATHS

Before learning how to do a U-turn in your snazzy new Bug-Out Vehicle, it's worth looking at exactly how the road users who died in previous zombie outbreaks met their end. The following chart is made up of data from the 3 major zombie outbreaks, all of which lasted more than 3 weeks, so it's the best information we have.

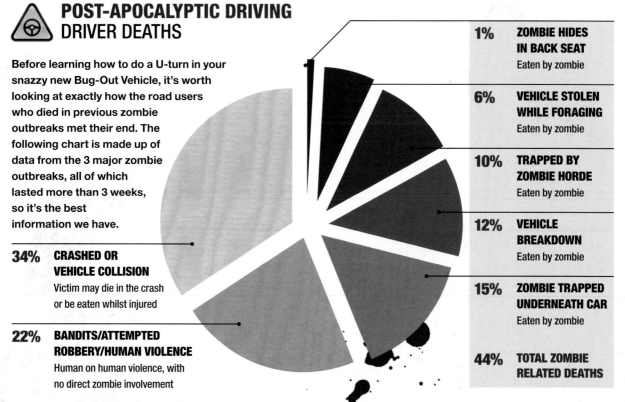

34% **CRASHED OR VEHICLE COLLISION**
Victim may die in the crash or be eaten whilst injured

22% **BANDITS/ATTEMPTED ROBBERY/HUMAN VIOLENCE**
Human on human violence, with no direct zombie involvement

1% **ZOMBIE HIDES IN BACK SEAT**
Eaten by zombie

6% **VEHICLE STOLEN WHILE FORAGING**
Eaten by zombie

10% **TRAPPED BY ZOMBIE HORDE**
Eaten by zombie

12% **VEHICLE BREAKDOWN**
Eaten by zombie

15% **ZOMBIE TRAPPED UNDERNEATH CAR**
Eaten by zombie

44% **TOTAL ZOMBIE RELATED DEATHS**

MINISTRY OF ZOMBIES

SOURCE: MINISTRY OF ZOMBIES OFFICE OF STATISTICS, BASED ON OUTBREAKS IN PERU 1984, THAILAND 2001, AND ITALY 2004.

POST-APOCALYPTIC ROAD CONDITIONS

1 BLOCKS, JAMS, AND ROADBLOCKS

By now you should be aware that the arrival of the zombies will see a mindless rush onto our roads as the crowds try to use their poorly maintained people carriers to flee the dead. Combine this with abandoned roadblocks and broken down vehicles and many carriageways will be impassable to most vehicles. You will need to start making a map early on. Some routes will be clear; some will be mangled no-go areas dominated by horrific uncleared crashes and clustered zombie populations.

2 DETERIORATING ROAD CONDITIONS

It is unlikely that the local council will continue filling in potholes after the end of the world and, as the seasons pass, expect things to get much more challenging on the roads. You'll be seeing more collapsed manhole covers, deep suspension-busting potholes and larger sinkholes. This will all be in addition to the everyday hazards of general debris and road wreckage. If you are planning on using a snazzy mid-life crisis sports car as your post-apocalyptic vehicle, then you may want to reconsider that 6 mm ground clearance at the front.

3 FLOODS

Water deserves a special mention here. Expect to encounter far more floods than normal as rivers burst their banks and fight back to their natural courses and leaks go unfixed. Remember, it's not as simple as driving through a shallow puddle. Never drive through water unless you know the maximum depths you will be facing. Also, hitting deep water at speed can be like crashing into a brick wall. Be cautious, plan your way around if necessary and avoid become a watery snack for any opportunistic ghouls.

4 TUNNELS, BRIDGES, AND COLLAPSES

Worth a special mention as many are such crucial parts of our transport infrastructure. How long do you trust a bridge for? Months, years? What about a dark tunnel? The latter is to be avoided at all costs. If you've seen any zombie movies then you will know that driving into a long dark tunnel rarely ends well. Over time, the danger of the undead will be replaced by collapses as maintenance schedules are abandoned and burning wrecks are left to do their damage. Our bridges may fair better – at least any danger should be more visible – but still approach with caution. As the years go by, expect structural faults to develop and for them to eventually become too dangerous to use.

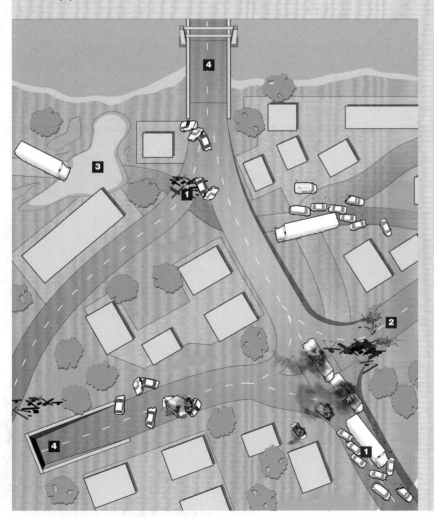

> **"THE FISCAL BUDGET FOR ZOMBIE SURVIVAL ROAD PLANNING HAS INCREASED BY $200 MILLION SINCE THE 2011 OUTBREAK. THAT'S DESPITE AN OVERALL REDUCTION IN THE BUDGET OF $250 MILLION SINCE THE AUSTERITY CUTS DURING FISCAL YEAR 2008–9 AND A 50% CUT IN ZOMBIE-PROOFING GRANTS."**
> **THE US HIGHWAYS AGENCY***

* A CONFUSING RESPONSE TO A FREEDOM OF INFORMATION REQUEST BY THE MINISTRY OF ZOMBIES IN APRIL 2017.

35

POST-APOCALYPTIC DRIVING

ZOMBIE AWARENESS

There are two general areas to consider – how to drive safely on roads dominated by the undead and then how you can safely use your vehicle to help humanity by reducing the number of dead on the roads. The first is the most important but the second one is far more interesting – who doesn't want to use their pimping post-apocalyptic vehicle to run zombies over?

First things first – this manual is about helping you prepare to get around in the wake of a zombie outbreak, and, for most, this will mean getting out there and enjoying our post-apocalyptic roadways. Secondly, although zombies don't drive (hopefully you already knew that), the millions of dead milling around will impact on your journey – whether you plan a short foraging trip or a major cross country relocation.

SURVIVOR OR ZOMBIE?

Everyone loves running down a zombie – it's a fact of life – but the activity is not without its dangers. Some survivors advocate avoiding it all together, others see it as a community-spirited and fun way to trim down their numbers. What is certain is that you need to be sure it's a zombie before you approach at ramming speed.

"CAUSING THE DEATH OF AN INFECTED INDIVIDUAL BY MEANS OF A VEHICLE IS BY NO MEANS CLEAR LEGALLY. ANY PRESIDING AUTHORITY WOULD NEED TO WEIGH THE DEGREE OF INFECTION OF THE VICTIM AGAINST THE VERY OBVIOUS BENEFIT OF WHACKING A FEW ZOMBIES."
GUIDO RAMOULDI, THE COURT OF HUMAN RIGHTS

▶ HOW TO CONTROL A CAR SKIDDING ON ZOMBIES

Cars skid for many reasons – in normal times, the main cause is braking too hard in wet conditions. Post-apocalyptic conditions certainly contain this danger but to this we should add what is technically known as "zombie road gunk."

WHAT IS ZOMBIE ROAD GUNK?
With thousands of dead on the roads, material from crushed body parts, including intestine content and internal body organs, will combine to create a highly viscous sludgy mess known as zombie road gunk.

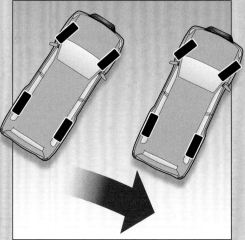

STEP 1
AVOIDANCE
Be aware of the road surface, particularly if you are running down groups of zombies. The threat will be higher in wet conditions for obvious reasons. Do not brake hard, slow down when hitting zombies and drive at an appropriate speed. This skill requires practice – it's about controlling your vehicle.

STEP 2
DON'T PANIC
If you feel your vehicle starting to slip, stay calm. Jamming your foot down on either the brake or the accelerator could see you ramming in to the nearest wall. First step is to gently ease up on the gas and attempt to regain control of the vehicle if possible. You may still be able to stop a total loss of control.

POST-APOCALYPTIC DRIVING
TIPS FOR CLIPPING THE DEAD

Safely "clipping" zombies in the wasteland not only provides a useful service to the rest of humanity, but it can also be a very therapeutic way to spend an afternoon during the "end times." But you need to bash the zombies in a safe and efficient way. These simple rules should guarantee hours of carefree zombie crushing.

1 Ensure that your vehicle is prepared for the wasteland, including frontal protection and meshed windows. Remember, your vehicle should be in "good working order."

2 You should aim to "clip" the zombie with the side of your vehicle unless it is purposely designed to run down and flatten the walking dead. Solder on some clipping wings with blades or spikes to increase the entertainment value of a hit.

3 Further enhance the fun and the drama by using games such as walking dead snooker. Be aware the zombies dressed in red become increasingly difficult to find so don't take risks just to get that stray ghoul.

4 Manage your speed carefully – you don't need masses of speed to be effective and it will only increase the risk of an accident. Don't become obsessed with hitting a particular zombie – there will be plenty out there for you. Sometimes, you'll just need to let it go.

5 Be patient and choose your targets carefully. You may be able to get higher points by identifying clusters of zombies. Be wary of hidden obstructions such as medians or you could find yourself being clipped by the dead.

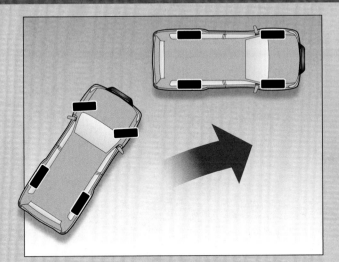

STEP 3
RECOVERING FROM A SKID

As the gas is eased, if the wheels skid to the right then gently steer in that direction. Use slight movements and the vehicle will begin to straighten up. (Reverse the steering direction as required for a skid to the left.) Again, these maneuvers require a cool head and calm thinking, which is tough if you have passengers panicking on-board.

STEP 4
BACK TO NORMAL

As the vehicle straightens, gently level up the steering wheel to leave the car looking forward. You may want to bring the vehicle to a stop if it's safe to do so to give yourself a breather. Always complete a quick perimeter check once your vehicle has come to a halt. Don't let it play over in your mind – there will be time for that later on. Now, it's about survival.

POST-APOCALYPTIC DRIVING

HIDDEN DANGERS

A crowd of zombies hanging around on the corner of a deserted high street is just asking to be run down but drivers beware as crowds or even lone zombies could be hiding any number of obstructions such as medians, large curbs, or even walls. They might look like a tempting target but if you're not sure, don't proceed. It is pointless incapacitating your vehicle, or worse, just to deal with a gang of rotting ghouls. The post-apocalyptic transport landscape will be a minefield of dangers, particularly on unexplored roads so ensure that you stay in "survival mode" as you drive through the wasteland. This is why experts only recommend 2 hours of apocalypse driving before taking a break. Your attention needs to be on at all times and your focus sharp. If possible, switch with another team member using a rotation system.

THE ZIG-ZAG FLIP

The Zig-Zag Flip is a reckless maneuver so common that it's even got its own name and is typically mentioned on every post-zombie apocalypse driving course when discussing what not to do on the roads during a zombie apocalypse. It involves hapless and over-excited drivers veering across roads trying to hit particular zombies, only for them to lose control of their vehicle and see it flip over. The situation sounds unlikely but experience of outbreaks has shown that it is a leading cause of zombie–related road traffic accidents (ZRTAs). No one likes to let a zombie get away and this sometimes leads drivers to take inappropriate risks as they try to catch that "old one with the funny hat" or the "lanky hippy with the backpack." Avoid becoming the next victim of the Zig-Zag Flip by always staying "frosty" at the wheel – never let emotion take over.

▶ HOW TO MANAGE A SCREEN BLOCKER

Most drivers enjoy running down zombies – it's one of the few pleasures of the wasteland and, most of the time, you can also enjoy the satisfying crunch as the dead are directed underneath the vehicle. Job done – another of the undead hordes dealt with as a service to humanity. However, on occasions a zombie will flip upwards and land on your windscreen blocking your view. The creature can become entangled and leave you struggling to see the road ahead so you need to know how to deal with Screen Blockers.

ACCESSING YOUR VEHICLE

Many new cars are designed with front crumple zones and other features to protect people in any collision scenario. This makes sense for normal times but you should assess the front area of your vehicle to determine whether it is likely to direct zombies over or under. Many survivalists fit full steel bull bars or angled grills to ensure that they don't create a steady flow of the dead over the hood. Ensure that the front of your vehicle is fit for zombie bashing before you start.

STEP 1
MANAGING THE SHOCK

Picture this – you're driving along mashing zombies under the wheel when suddenly you hear a loud bang and the car goes dark. The initial shock of a zombie blocking your screen can be enough to cause an accident. Your first reaction will be to brake hard but it's important that you manage any shock before making your move.

MINISTRY OF ZOMBIES

POST-APOCALYPTIC DRIVING
UNWANTED PASSENGERS

A less exciting danger but one which will probably take down more survivors than any other zombie road hazard – in the course of driving around the wasteland, you are bound to pick up stray zombies that either grab onto or become hooked onto your vehicle.

Varieties of zombie such as Undercar Exhaust Grabbers could become caught underneath, only to emerge once you are safely parked in your secure compound. You may find limbless wonders still grabbing on to the trunk after parking, ready to catch the unaware survivor. Remember, whenever you park your vehicle, listen for any groaning and complete a visual check before leaving. Don't let other survivors get caught by an oil-soaked ghoul you brought into a secure area.

WARNING!
THE MINISTRY OF ZOMBIES ADVISE CAUTION WHEN CHECKING

STEP 2
TAKING ACTION
Braking hard is useful as it will often send the zombie flying forward and clearing your windscreen but always check your mirrors first as, for example, if you are in a convoy, you could create a serious accident. Where possible, slow the vehicle without ramming on the brakes, bringing it to a controlled stop to avoid skidding.

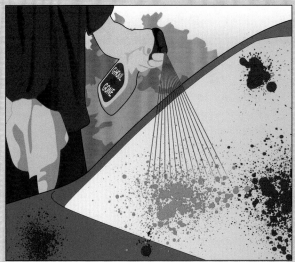

STEP 3
CLEARING UP
Once it's safe to do so, clear your windscreen of any zombie or body parts, being careful in case ghouls are present underneath the vehicle. Use a decent cleaner to clear off the gunk – water will often just leave you with a greasy mess of rotting body fluids.

POST-APOCALYPTIC DRIVING

HOSTILE HUMANS

You've read your zombie survival manual, you've got your base and transport sorted and you're cruising the wasteland in your ideal survival vehicle. Now for the bad news. There are plenty of not great folks out there who are going to want to take your stuff, your car and even your life. What you learned from your driving instructor may help you reverse into a parking space at Tesco but it won't cover high-speed getaways or pulling an emergency U-turn.

AMBUSHES

Expect no end of variation and tricks as they become more desperate and in some cases more organized. An "ambush" is any occasion when you're taken by surprise in your vehicle. Generally, experts recognize two main types:

▶ STATIC AMBUSH

This type involves you having to stop or go slowly through a "kill zone." Imagine armed gang organized ad-hoc roadblocks or check points at junctions or crossing points. Expect them to use deception, perhaps posing as soldiers or peaceful survivors. As law and order collapses, groups will spring up in some areas.

▶ ROLLING AMBUSH

This type happens on the move. For example, a vehicle might overtake with a gun firing off into the air. Their task is to distract you and get you to stop. Meanwhile, you'll be hemmed in from both behind and side by other supporting vehicles. Their objective is to take away your mobility. Once you stop, you'll be surrounded by armed assailants.

▶ HOW TO COMPLETE A U-TURN

You are bound to have seen a U-turn in various action movies – it's where the car reverses then pulls a complete 180 degree turn to keep driving in the same direction but without losing any speed. It's a hard maneuver to master but is invaluable if you need to reverse out of trouble in a hurry. A successful U-turn will enable you to make your escape and give you a head start over any intruders. Completing the move successfully in front of any bandits may be enough to convince them that you're not worth messing with.

STEP 1
REVERSE BACKWARDS

Scan your surroundings. You don't need lots of space but you do need to know you're not going to hit anything and can complete your spin. Throw the vehicle into reverse but keep looking forward. Pump the accelerator and get some speed up. It takes some practice but you should continue to look forward.

STEP 2
STEERING

Get one hand on the steering wheel at the 04.30 or 07.30 position depending on which way you are going spin and grab the gear shift with the other hand. Give the blocking bandits an icy stare and prepare to leave them gawping in admiration and, hopefully, some fear.

POST-APOCALYPTIC DRIVING
AVOIDING AN AMBUSH

The best ambush defence tactic is to avoid it in the first place. For the survival novice this can sound like a case of stating the bleedin' obvious but recognizing some of the signs can give you that vital early mover advantage.

SPOT THE DANGER EARLY

Be aware of the signs, always scan ahead and be suspicious of anyone else on the road. You'll soon develop a sixth sense for these things. Know when to avoid locations or roads.

STOPPING IN THE "KILL ZONE"

Whatever their objective, your opponents want to immobilize you in their prepared kill-zone so if at all possible avoid this. Use maneuvers such as the U-turn to buy you a fighting chance at making an escape.

USE CAR AND BODY ARMOUR

If your attackers are primarily interested in your loot, they may chance a few rounds into your vehicle so where possible use car armour and body armor – these could be a life-saver.

COUNTERING AN AMBUSH

Experienced drivers will tell you that there isn't a text book way to get out of an ambush. Every situation is different and you need to fall back on an arsenal of skills and techniques. Always expect a secondary ambush so your priority is to get out of the kill zone as quickly as possible.

You'll often hear experienced zombie fighters say that they just "don't like a particular set up" and move on. Learn to trust your gut even if it means missing out on some valuable loot.

STEP 3
GAS OFF, STEERING OVER

Let up on the gas and the weight of the vehicle will shift towards the rear. At the same time, yank the wheel as sharply as you can to induce the vehicle into a 180 degree spin. At this point, any survivors in your vehicle will be thrown from side to side so don't forget to tell them what you're planning. It's worth having a code phrase you can shout so as not to tip off any bad guys. Something simple such as "Momma likes the spice!"

STEP 4
MAKING YOUR ESCAPE

Once your vehicle is turning and once it hits 90 degrees, yank the steering wheel back into an upright position. If you get your timing right, you should be facing the other way with little reduction in speed and be able to make good your escape, leaving the breathless bandits with the choice to either pursue an obvious "hard nut" or just decide to let you go.

POST-APOCALYPTIC DRIVING

SURVIVOR GROUPS

As time progresses, the mix of who is on the road after a major zombie outbreak is going to change. The first few weeks will be dominated by unprepared survivors, desperate emergency services and the occasional remnants of a military unit. This period won't last long and soon you will find yourself sharing the post-apocalyptic roadway with a diverse array of potentially dangerous groups. It is vital that you consider the main survivor profiles and be able to recognize their vehicles and their battle tactics. The Ministry of Zombies developed a set of survivor profiles, which has since been adopted by many in the zombie survival community as an "industry-standard." As with any profiling, these are generalized and survivors will no doubt encounter mixed and hybrid groups. Nevertheless, these profiles are helpful, particularly in terms of your offensive and defensive driving tactics against such opponents.

"WE WILL ONLY START TO SEE THE EMERGENCE OF THE MORE ORGANIZED EXTREME GROUPS AROUND THREE MONTHS AFTER Z-DAY, WHEN THE LAST VESTIGES OF LAW AND ORDER AND SOCIETAL BARRIERS HAVE BEEN WELL AND TRULY BROKEN."
DR RAYMOND CARTER, PROFESSOR OF VIROLOGY

WITHIN ONE MONTH OF Z-DAY

Unprepared survivors, panicking individuals and any remaining military or police units. They will be scattering from the main urban centers, road chaos, ad-hoc looting, and outbreaks of violence on the roads.

ONE–THREE MONTHS AFTER Z-DAY

Opportunistic criminal gangs will become more organized, the remaining survivors will be more "zombie-hardened" and fragmented military or police units will disintegrate or transform. The great escape from urban centers is over. Looting is more organized. Vehicles will start to appear more adapted to the end of the world. Expect a large number of motorcycles as easily available fuel starts to become scarcer.

MORE THAN THREE MONTHS AFTER

Dominant criminal gangs will start to organize into structured robber baron groups. Hardcore wasteland warriors will remain but in too few numbers to defend survivors against any number of bizarre groupings such as cannibals and possibly mutants. This is when the true wasteland will emerge. Expect violent organised groups, battles over fuel and Mad Max-style innovations on the road. In many ways, the roads will be more dangerous than in the first weeks of the apocalypse.

HITTING THE ROAD
ENCOUNTERING SURVIVORS

Be particularly aware of any lone humans you come across as they may have been thrown out or escaped from their own party after becoming infected.

These dangerous individuals will be keen to try to integrate into your party and an enemy within is the most dangerous as they will already be within your security perimeter. They will disguise the fact that they are infected by either trying to blot it out or by hoping in vain for some kind of recovery. If they turn up at night, then they will cause serious problems for your party. Treat any newcomer with caution but also remember that they may genuinely be alone and could bring valuable new skills into your party. Just keep a close eye on them at first.

  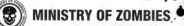

SURVIVOR GROUP PROFILES

	MOST LIKELY TO BE FOUND	THEIR TACTICS	YOUR TACTICS
The Great Unprepared "We don't need no help"	Aimlessly foraging, trying to find a way to survive. Most likely on foot or stolen BMX.	Typically passive. If they attack, it will be panicky, uncoordinated and desperate, particularly if they see your Bug-Out Gear and decide you look vulnerable enough.	Leave them in peace if you can. These lost souls are those unprepared for the end of the world and they've got enough on their plate. If they are foolish enough to attack, sit back and bat them away like flies.
Generation Zee "OMG! I am so gonna skin you alive!"	Hanging around post-apocalyptic corners, waiting for burnt out branches of McDonalds to re-open.	Swarm attacks, particularly on lone targets. Generation Z will always look for signs of weakness and will attack if they feel dissed. As the months progress, this group will become more unpredictable and violent.	Avoid eye contact, ensure that you are as big a target as possible and therefore costly to attack. Back away if necessary, ensuring that you cover your retreat. Do not confront or challenge unless you have over-whelming force. If in combat, target the ring-leaders.
Wasteland Warriors "I used to work in a call center"	Patrolling the wastelands and towns, often looking for some kind of mission.	These warriors will gravitate towards trouble then engage fiercely to defend helpless survivors. They will often pull surprise weapons from their vehicles and fight to the end.	Don't attack any helpless survivors while these drivers are around. Play it cool. A subtle nod of the head with perhaps an admiring glance will normally see you through. This group often has a plucky sidekick or sturdy dog.
Traveling Survivors "I'm outta water, let's be friends?"	Our crumbling motorways and A roads, heading for that elusive safe zone.	Will corral if attacked into an old-fashioned defensive circle. Expect the occasional firearm.	Convoys of traveler are unlikely to attack unless they're really desperate. As the months progress, those left will be battle-hardened and up for a fight if required. Avoid unless you want to be exposed to their extensive back story. You'll soon learn that everyone alive after the apocalypse has a story.
Robber Barons "I'll take those supplies"	Foraging warehouses, threatening survivor communities and generally trying to expand their "empires."	Full on, likely to have firearms, be battle-hardened and able to call on reinforcements. Likely to include some ex-military, tactics will be sophisticated and organised, such as flanking.	Avoid if at all possible. Stay away from their known territories, looting locations and bases. Don't steal their parking spaces. If you are captured, you are most likely be asked to pledge your allegiance. Robber Barons themselves typically carry some kind of token weapon like a cricket-bat covered in barbed wire.
Apocalypse Amazons "Multi-tasking to the end of the world"	The better shopping malls and city centers. Any boutique that hasn't been burnt out. Any coffee shops still open.	VW beetles, with post-apocalypse pimpage. Numerous small cars, with the occasional Chelsea tractor (premium SUV). This group doesn't typically attack but if do, expect an organised and swift swarm style assault.	You leave them alone, they'll leave you alone. Whatever you do don't tailgate an amazon convoy. If find them in a deserted high street, just let them finish. You can de-escalate any confrontation by directing them to an unlooted brand-name shop they may not be aware of.
Cannibals "You look so sweaty and tasty"	Either their settlements or known combat black spots. Cannibals also favor hospitals and other medical locations.	Will avoid conflict against stronger opponents. In combat, will leave vehicle attack with blunt and bladed weapons. Often fights as a family group so expect to be attacked by everyone from Granny to baby Caleb.	Be strong, try to look as powerful as possible and wear slimming clothes. Try not to look too tasty – for example, sweating profusely can give you that "just basted" look which cannibals find appetising. Equally, having long, greasy hair can ensure you look less appealing.
Ex-military/ Robocops "Respect my authority maggot!"	Key foraging locations such as warehouses, military bases and along their convoy routes.	Similar to Robber Baron groups but these guys are well-trained in close protection and vehicular combat. They are skillful drivers, typically working as part of a team.	Avoid if possible. Less trigger happy and ambitious than organised bandits but they may still liberate your vehicle if they fancy it. Do not appear to be a threat if you meet one of their convoys but keep one hand on your gun in case things get toasty.
End of the World Scientists "Quick, I've run out of test tubes!"	Mad loners, locked in their homes. If outside, they'll be found in some specialist supply or shops.	Mad loners avoid others by choice, unless they start some lunatic quest to "cleanse the earth" – which will probably happen at some point. If they do, expect something akin to the child-catcher from *Chitty Chitty Bang Bang*.	Will only attack if they absolutely have to or are driven to either by a need for supplies or the voices in their head. Their targets will be those alone or vulnerable. Be firm and make it known you are armed and both groups will think twice. If they are foraging for supplies, just leave them to it.

GLOSSARY

Ambush To attack by surprise from a hiding place.

Apocalypse The complete final destruction of the world.

Cannibal Animals that eat their own kind

Crossbow Bows mounted across wooden blocks.

Forage To hunt or search for something.

Ghoul A zombie or evil creature.

Infrared Light waves that are outside of the visible part of the light range at the red end, which we can see.

Maneuver A movement or series of moves requiring skill and care.

Navigation The act of guiding a vehicle, ship, or aircraft.

Pannier A basket or bag carried on a bicycle or beast of burden.

Survivalist A person who practices survival skills and tries to ensure their own survival.

 **MINISTRY OF ZOMBIES**

FOR FURTHER READING

Austin, John. *So Now You're a Zombie: A Handbook for the Newly Undead.* Chicago: Chicago Review Press, 2010.

Brooks, Max. *The Zombie Survival Guide: Complete Protection from the Living Dead.* New York: Crown Archetype, 2003.

Brooks, Max. *World War Z: An Oral History of the Zombie War.* New York: Crown Archetype, 2007.

Luckhurst, Roger. *Zombies: A Cultural History.* London: Reaktion Books, 2015.

Ma, Roger. *The Zombie Combat Manual: A Guide to Fighting the Living Dead.* London: Penguin Publishing Group, 2010.

FOR MORE INFORMATION

https://www.cdc.gov/phpr/zombie/index.htm

https://www.cnn.com/2014/05/16/politics/pentagon-zombie-apocalypse/index.html

https://www.forbes.com/sites/kevinmurnane/2017/01/08/guess-how-many-people-will-survive-a-zombie-apocalypse/#5801616c5e40

https://www.natgeokids.com/uk/discover/science/general-science/zombie-apocalypse-survival/

https://www.rei.com/blog/social/infographic-13-essential-tools-for-surviving-a-zombie-outbreak

INDEX

A

acceleration, 6, 12, 18
AK-47, 10, 19, 24
all-terrain vehicles (ATVs), 29
ambulances, 6
ambushes, 29, 40, 41
antibacterial wipes, 11
Apocalypse Amazons, 43
armor, 8, 9, 13, 14, 15, 17, 18,
    19, 24, 26, 27, 31, 41
audio tapes, 5

B

baseball bat, 10, 14, 16
BMW cruisers, 28
bridge collapses, 35
Bug-Out Kit/Bag, 10, 11, 17, 28, 31, 33
Bug-Out Route, mapping one, 33
Bug-Out Vehicle, how to outfit one, 7, 10, 11, 14
Bug-Out Zone, how to create one, 33
bulletproof glass, 9, 17, 19
buses, 6, 26–27

C

cannibals, 43
chainsaws, 18
chicken wire, 8
clipping, 37
color sensitivity, 8
C.R.A.Z. system, 34
crossbows, 14, 30, 31

D

decomposition filter, 12, 16, 17
directional lights, 8
doors, reinforcing them, 8
driver deaths, statistics on, 34
driving tips, 32–42

E

emergency bag, 10
emergency dental kit, 11
emergency vehicles, pros and cons of, 6
End of Days Caravans, 24
End of the World Scientists, 43
exhaust system, reinforcing it, 13
ex-military members, 43

F

fan belts, 11
fenders, reinforcing them, 8
firearms, 6, 8, 10, 14, 16, 17, 18, 19,
    24, 26, 30, 31, 43
first aid kit, 17
FITBOW maintenance system, 12
floods, 10, 35

folding bicycle, 10
foraging, 6, 7, 10, 14, 19, 20, 22,
    27, 28, 29, 30, 33, 36, 43
4-wheel drive, 6
front bumper, reinforcing, 9
fuel, where to forage for it, 20–21
fuel economy/efficiency, 7, 8, 28, 30
fuel stabilizers, 10
fuses, 11

G

garage, how to fortify one, 22, 23
gas can, 10, 17, 20, 22, 26, 27
Generation Zee, 43
Great Unprepared, 43
grenades, 19, 30
ground clearance, 6, 13, 28, 31, 35

H

handcart, 10
hatchbacks, pros and cons of, 6
helmets, importance of, 31
hiding place, 23
Honda Gold Wing, 28
Humvee, 8
Hyundai Veloster Turbo, 18

I

inflatable boat, 10
infrared camera, 27

J

jumper cables, 11

K

Kel-Tec-KSG, 31
kill zone, 40, 41

L

Leyland Supra-Diesel Engine, 26
Liberty "Freedom" Wasteland Chopper, 30, 31
light proofing, 23
looting, 14, 20, 21, 22, 31, 41, 42, 43

M

maps, 11, 19, 27, 33, 35
mini-bikes, pros and cons of, 28
moped, pros and cons of, 28
M60, 8, 14, 15, 16, 17, 18, 19, 24
Multicat Zombiecross 60
    "The Winchester," 24, 25
music, 5

MINISTRY OF ZOMBIES

N

navigation system, 11, 19, 27
Negev machine gun, 19

O

off-road bikes, pros and cons of, 29
off-road driving, 6, 7, 13, 19, 26, 28, 29, 30, 32

P

passenger space, 6, 7, 29
pepper spray, 10
pickup trucks, pros and cons of, 7
police baton, 10
police cars, 6
prescription medicine, 11

Q

quiet, importance of, 13

R

Range Rover, 8, 21
razor wire, 22
"ready-to-eat" rations, 11, 19
rear-flame tail gun, 14, 15, 16, 17, 20
recreational vehicles (RVs), 24–25
Remington Model 887, 31
roadblocks, 29, 35, 40
road conditions, 6, 24, 28, 35
road cruisers, pros and cons of, 28
road utility vehicles (RUVs), pros and cons of, 7
Robber Barons, 43
robocops, 43
rolling ambush, 40
roof, reinforcing it, 8
roof mounted machine gun, 14, 15, 19
Routemaster Apocalypse Bus, 26–27
Royal Jordanian Automotive Consortium, 18

S

scooters, pros and cons of, 28
Screen Blockers, 32, 38
skidding, 36, 37, 39
skid plates, 13
sleeping bags, 11
smoke bombs, 19
sound proofing, 23
spare tire, 10, 22
speed, 6, 12, 16, 18, 20, 24, 25, 26, 28, 29, 30, 35, 36, 37, 40, 41
sports cars, pros and cons of, 6
sport utility vehicles (SUVs), pros and cons of, 7
static ambush, 40
stealing, 6, 7, 28, 43
steel grill, 8

steel shutters, 9
storage, 5, 6, 7, 8, 11, 7, 19, 23, 25, 27, 28, 29, 30, 31
survivor groups, types of, 42–43
SWAT team vehicles, 6

T

Tennessee Motorcycle Company, 30
tires, types of, 8
Toyota Hilux Invincible, 7, 18
Traveling Survivors, 43
trikes, pros and cons of, 28

U

Undercar Exhaust Grabbers, 39
U-turn, 32, 34, 40, 41

V

vans, 6
vehicle maintenance, 12, 22
vehicle weight, 12, 13, 14, 17, 24, 30, 41

W

walkie-talkies, 19
walking dead snooker, 37
Wasteland Warriors, 43
water purification kit, 10
wheel blades, 8
windshields, reinforcing them, 8, 9

Z

Zig-Zag Flip, 38
Zombie Apocalypse Kit (Z-poc Kit), 25
zombie awareness, importance of while driving, 36
zombie-related road traffic accidents (ZRTAs), 38
zombie road gunk, 12, 25, 31, 36, 39
zombie scoop, 17
zombie whistles, 8, 19
ZOM 90E Road Warrior, 18, 19